Man *and*
Economics

Robert A. Mundell
Professor of Economics
University of Chicago

Man *and* Economics

McGraw-Hill Book Company
New York, St. Louis, San Francisco, Toronto, London, Sydney

In memory of W. R. M.

Man *and* Economics

Library of Congress Catalog Card Number 68–13522

34567890 BABA 74321069

Preface

Economics is the science of choice. It began with Aristotle but got mixed up with ethics in the Middle Ages. Adam Smith separated it from ethics, and Walras mathematized it. Alfred Marshall tried to narrow it, and Keynes made it fashionable. Robbins widened it, and Samuelson dynamized it, but modern science made it statistical and tried to confine it again.

But the science won't stay put. It keeps cropping up all over the place. There is an economics of money and trade, of production and consumption, of distribution and development. There is also an economics of welfare, manners, language, industry, music, and art. There is an economics of war and an economics of power. There is even an economics of love.

Economics seems to apply to every nook and cranny of human experience. It is an aspect of all conscious action. Whenever decisions are made, the law of economy is called into play. Whenever alternatives exist, life takes on an economic aspect. It has always been so. But how can it be?

It can be because economics is more than just the most developed of the sciences of control. It is a way of looking at things, an ordering principle, a complete part of everything. It is a system of thought, a life game, an element of pure knowledge.

It is also useful in many ways, as the rest of this book tries to show.

Robert A. Mundell

Contents

I. *Principles*

1. *The Law of Economy*

Economics is concerned with want and resources. It examines that aspect of individual and social action by which resources are used to reduce want. Because want is a state of mind, economics deals with *man*. Because resources constitute matter, economics deals with *nature*. Man and want, nature and resources—these are the universal actors in the drama of economics.

The ingredients of drama are in every economic problem, if by drama is meant, as in the great tragedies of the theater, the confrontation of opposing forces. In economic problems there is always the confrontation of opposing forces: want and resources, desire and opportunity, man and nature, consumption and saving, supply and demand. The act of choice is but the final act, the denouement, where the romantic forces of desire are pitted against the realistic forces of opportunity.

There is no way of knowing whether man or nature is the more basic concept of economics. Man is part of nature, and therefore man is lesser. But nature is a postulate of man's perception, and therefore man is greater. Any attempt to establish the priority of one concept over the other meets with a metaphysical contradiction.

Want is basic to economics. It plays an essential role in the consumption process, and consumption is, as Adam Smith said, the sole end and purpose of all production. Without want there would be no basis for choice, no grounds for decisions, no purpose to consumption. Man would be a vegetable, purposeless and pointless. But want is indeed unlimited. It is ubiquitous, universal, and eternal. It springs from man's knowledge of himself, from the time he tasted the forbidden fruit. It springs from man's ignorance, from the primordial instincts that make him a biological entity. Want is a bottomless pit, and between the Garden of Eden and heaven its absence is not conceivable.

Resources derive from nature. They play the enabling role in the production process. Without resources nothing could live, and there would be no basis for perceiving the existence of anything else. There would be a nothingness, in itself beyond comprehension. But resources are limited. Matter is limited, and space is finite. Abundance of everything is a meaningless concept, beyond the purview of man and outside the objectivity of his existence. *Nothing* is unlimited.

Want, being a state of mind, is an attribute of subjective man, and so economics has an origin in the *psychological sciences.* Resources, being a state of nature, are an attribute of matter, and so economics has an origin in the *physical sciences.* The economic aspects of the sciences are joined in the transformation of matter into want elimination through the production and consumption of *goods.* The subjective and objective phenomena of life are joined in the economic concept of goods.

Resources constitute the class of all things that exist, wants the class of desired things that are lacking. Goods are desired things that exist, an overlapping of the class of wants with the class of resources.

Resources that are not desired, that are not capable of satisfying desires or eliminating wants, are not goods; and neither are desired things that do not exist. There is no useful sense in which a flea on the planet Mars can be considered a good, since it is not (as far as we know) desired, nor is there any useful sense in which immortality can be considered a good, since it does not exist.

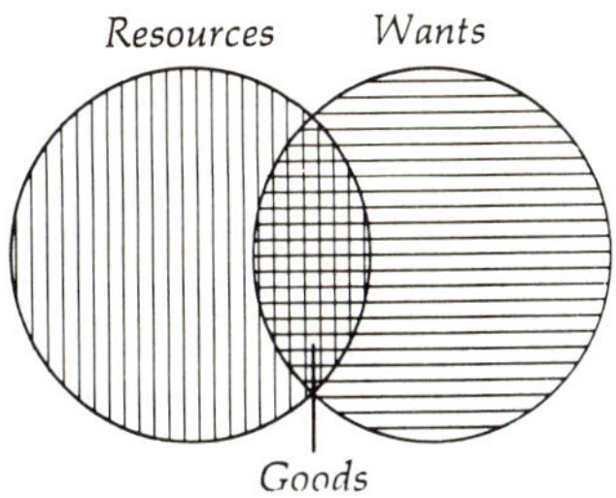

Hunger is a want, and food is a resource. Hunger creates the desire for food. Thus the availability of food for reducing hunger, combined with the ability to eat it, implies that food is a good. Available food, drink, and shelter are goods that can eliminate hunger, thirst, and cold; a symphony concert is a good that can satisfy a listener's love of music; and a toy train is a good that can satisfy a child's taste for play.

The concept of a good in economics is a very broad one. A loaf of bread is a good; and so are a car, a house, a painting, a Beatles record, a bed, and a dog. So might be air, a date with a girl, a swim in the sea, a conversation with a genius, and a beautiful sunset.

There are many different types of goods in economics. There are

Free goods, scarce goods
Goods made for market
Public goods, private goods
Goods made in Chile.

There are necessaries, luxuries
Snob goods of Veblen
There are war goods, peace goods
Goods sent to Vietnam.

There are present goods, future goods
Consumer goods and capital
Wholesale goods and wholesome goods
Goods not for children.

There are stolen goods, hot goods
Used goods and services
Intermediate goods and final goods
Goods made for retail.

Dry goods, Hong Kong goods
Import goods with taxes
Traded goods, home goods
Goods made with axes.

Substitutes, complements
Bread, butter, and cheese
Superior goods, inferior goods
Goods made for deepfreeze.

Outputs, inputs
Goods and factors
Inventions, patents
Plays by actors.

Goodness!

A good is a thing that directly affects enjoyment. However, some things subtract from enjoyment. We could, therefore, distinguish between goods and bads or positive goods and negative goods. But we can equally well make use of the fact that deprivation of a good is the mirror image of it. Instead of saying that clean air is a good and dirty air is a bad, we can say that clean air in some cities is a *scarce* good.

Scarcity is a central concept in economics. A scarce good is one that is not free in the sense that nobody has to pay for it. In an uncrowded world, gifts of nature such as scenery, water, clean air, privacy, and space are free. But as the world fills up with factories, automobiles, and people, these gifts become scarce; they cannot be had in unlimited quantities and are no longer free. Streams and lakes become polluted with sewage, city air absorbs factory smoke and exhaust fumes, virgin mountain slopes become crowded with ski lifts and crowds, and privacy and freedom diminish in the complexity of an indifferent social life.

The economic concept of scarcity has to be kept distinct from the physical fact that resources are limited. The water in the Atlantic Ocean is limited, for example, but it is not scarce, and likewise air in the atmosphere is limited but not scarce. Scarcity is not an attribute of a good, but the reflection of a situation, the interplay between wants and resources. In contrast to a free good, which can be enjoyed without giving up another good, a scarce good is one that can only be enjoyed by sacrificing the enjoyment of another good.

The concept of scarcity would exist even if physical resources were not limited. For there are, inherent in man, limits on his ability to consume and enjoy. Even if a man had all the money he could possibly use, his activity would be conditioned by scarcity. He would still have to allocate his time if only because life is limited. In choosing a meal, a man has to take account of the fact that his stomach is limited even if he is rich enough to ignore the expense of buying the meal. Life is always conditioned by the fact that time is irreversible and scarce and by limitations on the number of activities that can be pursued at the same time. Scarcity, therefore, gives rise to the act of choice.

Choice is selection from "alternatives." The word itself suggests scarcity. Choice implies two things. It implies a set of things that are available, called *opportunities.* And it implies a criterion of selection called *preferences.* The act of rational choice is the act of selecting the *best,* the most *preferred,* opportunity.

What are preferences? They are a ranking of things according to a criterion of selection. Preferences imply that the enjoyer—the entity making the choice, whether an individual or group—has an interest, but not necessarily a selfish interest, to maximize. An individual may want to maximize "happiness," "utility," "well-being," "enjoyment," or "virtue"; call it what you will. A business firm may want to maximize profits, the capital value of the firm, or the well-being of the managers or owners. A government may want to maximize social welfare or the power of the state or to minimize social tension. On the most general level, preferences imply only that the entity can rank desires in an order according to the degrees of enjoyment their satisfaction would provide.

Rational choice implies more than this, however. It also implies that the entity not only can but *will* select the most desired opportunity and that the ranking of desires into preferences is done in a noncontradictory way. Thus if a man prefers A to B and B to C, then he will be inconsistent if he does not also prefer A to C. If a man prefers a redhead to a blonde and a blonde to a brunette, surely he also prefers the redhead to the brunette. If he said he preferred the brunette to the redhead, he would contradict himself.

In simple choices, rational men and groups do not contradict themselves, but in complex decisions, groups and even individuals can be placed in positions where they do contradict themselves. This possibility is of great importance, not only in analyzing schizophrenic behavior and in formulating appropriate structures for government decision making but also in dealing with quite common contradictions within the human personality. Complex decision-making procedures of any entity may involve contradictions, as we shall see in Chapter 18.

The act of choice is the action of making a decision. A chooser is a decision maker. He confronts aspirations with limitations, preferences with opportunities, intentions with resources.

The act of choice integrates the psychological categories of wants, desires, and preferences with the objective categories of resources, goods, and opportunities. Wants (which are passive) produce desires (which are active), and desires are transformed into preferences; resources produce goods, and goods are transformed into opportunities. Preferences are joined with opportunities in the act of choice.

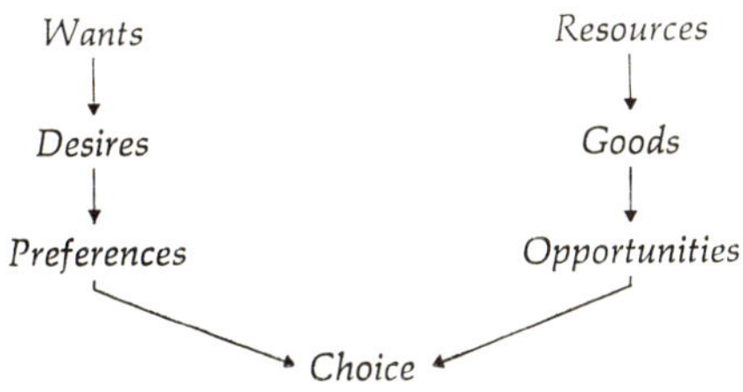

The act of rational choice leads to the law of economy. This law states that a given benefit will be achieved at the lowest cost; of things yielding equal satisfaction, rationality implies choice of the cheapest. The corollary is that at a given cost the best will be chosen; among things costing the same, rationality means choice of that which yields the most satisfaction. You never pay more for a particular thing than you have to. You find the highest market for something you want to sell, the cheapest for something you want to buy.

The law of economy is the basic postulate of economics and indeed a basic law of all human activity. It means that of two equal qualities of gasoline you would buy the cheapest. It means that if two colleges charged the same tuition, you would choose to enter that which you thought was better adapted to developing your talents and satisfying your social interests. It means that a government choosing among weapons systems that cost the same will choose the one it believes to be most effective. It means that a composer choosing among notes will select those which produce the greatest effect and that an author choosing a word will select the most effective one in his vocabulary.

Simple, obvious, even trivial though this principle seems, it yields tremendous insight into economic behavior and into fundamental problems of real life. Despite its simplicity—indeed, because of its simplicity—the law of economy gives us invaluable insight into how goods should be produced, distributed, and consumed, how defense strategy should be organized, how a work of art should be arranged, and even how a bride should be chosen!

2. *Transactions and Specialization*

Robinson Crusoe, trapped on his island, had no chance to engage in transactions. The things he wanted to consume he had to make himself. He was self-sufficient and autarkic, forced to adapt consumption to production. In his lonely circumstances transactions and exchange had no meaning for him.

Modern man, however, lives in a crowded world, with the benefits and inconveniences large crowds imply. People possess different abilities and resources, and they want to consume goods in different proportions. Different tastes and endowments give rise to diversity, and diversity opens up the possibility of profitable trade. People find it profitable to trade the things they possess in overabundance for the things they want more urgently. The act of trade is the act of making transactions.

A transaction is an exchange of two things. Something is given up, and something is got back. When you buy a book, you give up money and get back a book; when you work in a factory, you give up effort and get back money; when you borrow from a bank, you commit yourself to pay a sum of money in the future in return for a sum of money in the present.

Transactions may or may not involve monetary phenomena. You make a transaction when you exchange a ride in a car for a piano lesson. Conversation is an exchange of amusement or information. A treaty is an exchange of concessions or commitments. Love is an exchange of pleasures. The price of an object or group of objects is what is given up for it.

A price is implicit in all transactions. The price *per unit* is the *ratio* of what is given up to what is received. The money price of a book is the money given up for it, and the price of a treaty is the concession made for the benefits received.

It is useful, as well as conventional, to use a common money in which to denote the price, or terms, of a transaction. You may barter a car for ten cows or two sets of golf clubs for a pair of skis; but it is much more convenient to price everything in terms of money, for reasons I will elaborate in detail in Chapter 6.

This is not to say that it is easy to state the terms of all transactions as a price. Certainly not as a price expressed in terms of money. Some transactions involving honor, reputation, virtue, and other "sacred" aspects of life have no price—or only a very high price. The money price may be inoperative because the transaction is outside the realm of ordinary transactions. Of course you could always defend the cynic's truism "There is a price for everything" by saying the price for something a man will refuse to sell is infinite. But that is shibboleth circumlocution, an evasion of ordinary discourse for the sake of preserving a tautology.*

But it is extremely important to try and see how inclusive is the class of things that we call transactions. Money purchases,

* In Chap. 18 we shall have occasion to consider briefly this problem in a more fruitful way. The statement that everything has a price when infinity is included as one of the possible prices, is not scientifically useful or, indeed, meaningful, since it does not admit the possibility of making distinctions between two or more objects the price of which is infinite even when, by a different approach, meaningful distinctions are possible. A more fruitful approach is to discuss such questions in the context of so-called lexicographic utility functions in which priorities are explicitly introduced.

barter trades of physical objects, and exchange of information and enjoyments are readily seen as transactions. But what about gifts?

I have said that a transaction always has two sides to it, the ratio of the two sides being the price. Whether a gift is a transaction, therefore, is a matter of whether a gift has two sides to it. Is there a useful sense in which a gift has only one side to it, or is a gift merely an implied transaction in which the current transfer of an object from one party to another demands a subsequent, or has implied an antecedent, *quid pro quo?*

To explore this interesting question in detail would take us far into the realms of psychology, history, and anthropology and outside the scope of relevance. But a good prima facie case can be made for treating all gifts as implied transactions.

In the historical development of primitive societies gift exchange and ceremonial displays were among the earliest forms of trade. Gifts are tendered in different ways, but

> . . . no matter how freely a gift may be tendered, or how unsought it may be, the very fact of its having been presented carries an obligation of equivalent or increased return that can be ignored only on penalty of social disapprobation and the loss of prestige. Psychologically, this principle holds for all cultures. In the less specialized economies, however, where it commonly takes institutionalized form, it is of primary economic importance.*

In some primitive cultures, the exchange of gifts constitutes a major form of trade. A gift is given up, and a gift is got back, the implicit unit price of the transaction being the ratio of the

* H. G. Herskovits, *Economic Anthropology*, 1940, p. 155. The quotation is a translation from an earlier work of Marcel Mauss.

two gifts. But gift exchange need not be synchronous. The return gift may take place long after the original gift was tendered. Ceremonial displays in primitive cultures are means of buying prestige, the amount of prestige attained by any celebration depending on, say, the number of pigs or cows allotted to the slaughter. The payment is made at the time of the display; the repayment in the form of prestige is received later on.

Gift exchange may not therefore imply a contemporaneous *quid pro quo,* and that is perhaps the origin of the idea that gifts are not genuine transactions. If the thing received is not acquired at the time payment is made, the exchange is a more complicated one involving a trade and a credit transaction simultaneously. In societies using the system of gift exchange the receipt of a gift imposes an obligation to reciprocate, and the longer the time interval that lapses before reciprocation is effected, the greater the reciprocal gift should be, other things being equal, to take account of implicit interest charges.

Dowries are a form of ritualized exchange where, in some societies, the dowry is regarded either as the price the bride's family is willing to pay for being relieved of the bride's support or as a down payment on support for the bride's family in their old age. In some Moslem societies, on the other hand, the bridegroom makes a payment to the bride's family as security for the wife against divorce, a system by which the terms of divorce are arranged in advance.

Social security is a modern manifestation of what used to be gift exchange. Social security payments, as they have worked out in most countries, involve a payment from the working generation to the aged. As the three-generation family was superseded in the twentieth century by the two-generation family, the aged were left increasingly alone, creating the need for social security to accomplish, through impersonal cooperative activities, what had formerly been effected through a more elaborate family structure and kinship system.

The concept of transactions is therefore a very broad one. But we now have to see what it is that determines the nature of the objects exchanged. What is it that determines which goods are traded? Why do some countries produce some things, other countries other things? Why do countries like Switzerland specialize in the production and export of watches or machine tools, while countries like Australia or Argentina specialize in the production and export of mutton, wool, or beef?

The answer is that countries, regions, and people specialize because it is to their advantage to do so, and they specialize in those activities where the gains from specialization are greatest. The best way to see the advantage of trade is to envisage the circumstances that would prevail in its absence. Suppose, for example, that Australia, with its abundant resources of land, could produce a great quantity of agricultural products. To be specific suppose that if it applied all its resources to *agricultural* production, Australia could produce $20 billion worth of agricultural products valued at world-market prices, whereas if it devoted all its resources to manufactures, it could produce only $10 billion worth. If Australia specialized entirely in manufactures, its total produce would be worth only $10 billion, whereas if it specialized entirely in agricultural products, its total produce would be double that amount.

Now if Australia were an isolated country (in terms of trade), it would have to restrict its consumption to its production, so that if it wanted to consume both agricultural and manufactured goods, it would have to produce some of each. The result would be that Australia's income would be somewhere between $20 billion and $10 billion, depending on the proportion in which Australians wanted to consume agricultural and manufactured products. If, for example, the country divided its resources equally between each group, its income would be $15 billion, with production and consumption of agricultural goods accounting for $10 billion and production and consumption of manufactured goods accounting for $5 billion.

If now, however, we suppose the opening up of trade between Australia and the rest of the world, Australia can specialize entirely in agriculture. It can produce $20 billion worth of agricultural products and export the excess of production over consumption for imports of manufactures. By this means Australia can increase its income from the $15 billion prevailing in the absence of trade to the $20 billion possible under free trade, a total gain of $5 billion. As a result of trade with the rest of the world Australians can increase their total income and consumption by $5 billion. We can then say that Australia has an advantage in the production of agricultural products relative to manufactures, or a *comparative advantage* in the production of agricultural goods. The principle of comparative advantage in this context means that Australia can gain by specializing in agriculture.

What holds for Australia holds for every other country. The gains from trade explain why it is that countries throughout the world generally specialize in producing those goods their resources and the talents and skills of the population best equip them for. Thus Japan, with its large and relatively skilled population relative to land, is especially efficient in the production of light manufactures—radios, phonographs, cameras, and precision equipment—but finds it advantageous to import raw materials and food. India, with a large but relatively unskilled population and a small stock of capital, tends to be more efficient in the production of textiles and particular crops like jute, tea, and rice. Countries like Canada, on the other hand, with rich natural resources have an advantage in specializing in the export of minerals, wheat, and lumber products and, recently, because of the accumulation of capital, a growing list of manufactured products.

What holds for entire countries holds also for the regions of a country. In the United States, the West specializes in grain production, the East in manufactures, the South in cotton and other products, and the Midwest in dairy products and corn. Different regions of a country as large and diverse as the United States have different comparative advantages because the endowments of land, labor, capital, and skills are differently distributed throughout the country.

What holds for regions also holds for individuals, who in their daily lives specialize in those fields of endeavor in which they possess a comparative advantage. Again, we can notice that individuals enter into market transactions at all only because it promises to be profitable. Because a trader always has the possibility of withdrawing from the market—becoming like Robinson Crusoe—he will be willing to trade only if trade will make him better off than he would be without trade. He will trade only if the bundle of goods he can get through trade is worth more to him than the bundle he had available to him before trade.

How does one decide which goods to sell and which to buy? Given the prices on the market, a trader will sell those goods he values at less than the market price and buy those goods he values at more than the market price. As a machinist, for example, you would have little use for your own services at home, and so you would value your own consumption of your own services at much less than the wage offered for them in the market—at least compared to the value you would place on the food, clothing, housing, concerts, and television programs which you are not suited to provide for yourself.

But how does one get the stock of goods available for trade to start with? How did you acquire the machinist's services you are now able to sell?

One answer—an overly simplified one—is that you were *endowed* with them, either by heredity or training. But training is itself something that can be acquired on the market, and if you possess certain skills, you must have learned them or acquired them in anterior exchanges.

It is much more to the point, therefore, to find out how the goods a trading entity possesses are acquired. We will go into this in much greater detail in Chapter 7, but an introduction to the idea at this stage may be helpful. Take a student graduating from high school and about to embark on a career. We could suppose that he has a sum of money or the credit-worthiness to borrow money on his own abilities (from a bank, a university, the state, or friends). He first notices that he is sufficiently gifted to succeed in a university career, so that floating a loan (in effect selling a claim on part of his future income) in exchange for education at the university is itself a profitable trade. What subject will he take up?

After a period of time investigating the range of subjects in his beginning years and learning which subjects he excels in, he will make a choice based on his interests, aptitudes, and a consideration of the market potential for the training he chooses to acquire.

There may be a course at the university in basket weaving. He may be good at it; he may enjoy it; he may wish to do basket weaving all his life. But he is unlikely to specialize in it if he has explored his likely prospects as a basket weaver. The rewards from such an occupation are unlikely to be sufficient to give him a very high rate of return on his investment in education.

He may enjoy mathematics but not be good at it. He may be good at chemistry but not enjoy it. But he may find himself very good at biology and enjoy it, and very good at history and enjoy it. So he reduces his range of choice to those two subjects and chooses the one at which he *excels by the greatest margin.* Thus if he decides that he is likely to make a brilliant career in history but only a mediocre one in biology, he may decide on a career as a history teacher on the expectation that he will excel in that field by a greater margin. This is an application of the principle of comparative advantage to an individual.

But we can be more precise. A man will produce that good in which he has a comparative advantage, and he will have a comparative advantage in producing that good rather than another when the ratio of his productivity in producing it to his productivity in producing the other good exceeds or at least equals the ratio in the market.

After he has received his training, our history teacher will have a comparative advantage in that subject and "export" his services for the goods he wants to consume, because his productivity in producing his services as a history teacher will exceed his productivity in producing other things compared to the market. At a given moment of time his comparative advantage is given, but the process of training and education is at least partly a process of developing comparative advantages.

The direction of specialization depends on innate endowments. Small men do not specialize in becoming professional football players, men of average intelligence do not become research scientists, and so on. On the other hand, beautiful girls often become models or movie stars; extroverts often become successful salesmen; and strong, well-coordinated men occasionally become athletes. There is a process of selection by which comparative advantages are developed on the basis of natural endowments.

The goods people sell usually are made by processes using a high proportion of the skills they are gifted in, whereas the goods people buy usually are made by processes they are comparatively ungifted in. This principle applies to all levels of economic life and life in general. We have seen its application to the goods a nation produces. Countries in equatorial climates export tropical fruits because a warm climate is an essential ingredient in growing fruit. Less obviously, countries with cheap labor resources, like India, export products which use a relatively large amount of labor, such as textiles. Countries like Canada, Australia, and Argentina, with large endowments of land, export goods like cattle, wheat, and wool, since these goods require large quantities of land for their efficient production. Countries like Switzerland, with a highly skilled labor force, export precision instruments and watches because these goods require highly skilled labor, which over generations has become relatively plentiful in Switzerland.

Specialization and the principle of comparative advantage apply to the division of labor within the family. A wife may do the cooking, and her husband may sell his services as a machinist. But even if the husband is a better cook than his wife, she may still do the cooking, since the diversion of a machinist's time from his job could reduce the net income of the family as a whole; while he may be both a better cook and a better machinist than his wife, he has a comparative advantage as a machinist. Similarly, a high-paid business executive may find it preferable to hire a chauffeur to drive his wife around than do so himself, even if he drives a car better than the chauffeur. It is comparative advantage that determines the course of profitable trades.

3. *Choice and Optimization*

We have taken for granted, up to now, that the individual is willing to trade when transactions can make him better off. But trade involves decision making, and the process of decision making is complicated. The act of choice is not a simple activity. It may take a great deal of research to discover the range of opportunities—what is available—and considerable thought or soul-searching to find out one's preferences. There is, however, a standard sequence inherent in any act of choice.

The first step is to contemplate the field of all conceivable possibilities; this is called the *field of choice.* All courses of action are included, but of course the practiced chooser, armed with the experience of past choices and human intelligence, will narrow in an instant the field of choice to relevant possibilities. If you go into a restaurant to choose a meal, you are likely to contemplate particular types of food, say, oysters, lobster, a vintage wine, steak, liver, and ice cream, and the money they will cost; you will be able to banish in an instant considerations totally irrelevant to the choice problem confronting you, considerations such as the election of a president, your feelings about a particular work of art, or whether your car needs a tune-up.

The next step is to find out what is actually available and what you can afford. You get a menu and see that oysters are out of season and that the restaurant does not serve lobster. Also certain wines may be ruled out because you lack the money in your pocket to pay for them and cannot make use of a credit device, such as a credit card. All the things that are within the range of your possibilities constitute your *opportunity set*—the batch of all things available. One of the alternatives, of course, is to order nothing, so that doing nothing is one of the elements of your opportunity set.

The next problem is to see which elements in your field of choice would make you happier than you are in your present hungry state. These will probably include most things on the menu, but you may detest liver and prefer eating nothing to eating that. You may also rule out an expensive vintage wine, not because you wouldn't enjoy it or don't have the cash in your pocket to pay for it, but because buying it would mean giving up spending the money on something you might want to spend the money on at a later date.

The final step is to select the best point in the set of opportunities—the most preferred element. This is simply a mental process of trial and error. By introspection you arrive at a selection that leaves no possibility of further gain. You will then have reached a point of equilibrium, your choice, the *optimum*. You will have carried out the process of optimization.

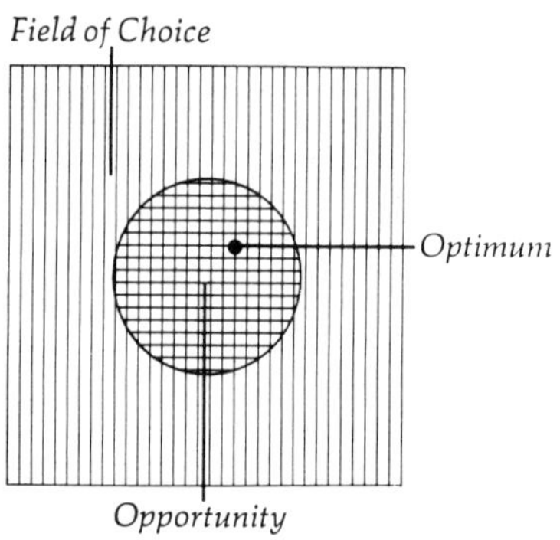

Choice typically results in a kind of *balance*. Indeed, balance is one of the most remarkable aspects of all life, a characteristic of activity so widespread that the term "unbalanced" has a pejorative ring to it. An unbalanced diet is not a good diet, an unbalanced mind is not a healthy mind, and an unbalanced painting has something wrong with it.

This astonishingly regular aversion to imbalance has an origin in a basic economic law, one I have already used in the discussion of problems of choice. When applied to consumption, it is called *the law of diminishing utility,* and when applied to production, *the law of diminishing productivity.* These terms, however, merely represent different applications of a general law, *the law of diminishing returns.*

The law of diminishing utility asserts that additional quantities of goods yield successively smaller increments of satisfaction. If we start out with a certain quantity of a good, units of which are ranked in the order of their desire-satisfying ability, and then acquire an additional quantity of the good, the increment may increase our satisfaction, but not to the same extent as did previous increments. An additional glass of milk, another pint of beer, a second car, a third apple, one more armchair—each will satisfy less urgent desires than its predecessor. Satiation will eventually set in.

The law of diminishing productivity is strictly analogous to the law of diminishing utility. It asserts that additional quantities of one of the factors of production—land, labor, materials, capital, management—will produce successively smaller increments of output when the other factors are held constant. The more tools or machines a worker has to work with, the greater his productivity; but after a point additional tools are no further help; the *marginal productivity* of the tools or machines falls. Similarly, the more effort expended in working a plot of land, the greater will be the output of the land (up to a point), but the less will be the added production of additional increments of work. Ten men working an acre of land will be able to produce more than one man on the same acre, but far less than ten times the product of the one man. It is for this reason that a farmer will employ a second hired man at less urgent tasks than the first and a third at less urgent tasks than the second; and he will use a second tractor or an additional stretch of fence to less advantage than the first.

The law of diminishing returns is a general law applicable to every conceivable subject. It applies in directions apparently far removed from the usual applications of economics—aesthetics, religion, physics, war. To make an example from the field of aesthetics, consider a music lover and his favorite piece of music. We have often heard music lovers say, "I could listen to that piece endlessly." But is it true? Of course not. Even allowing for changes in taste over time, satiation can and will set in. The same applies visually. In exaggeration of his aesthetic appreciation or as an advertisement of snobbishness, someone might imagine he could use his time indefinitely appreciating art, beautiful women, sunsets, mountain scenery. But the inexorability of the law makes itself felt. Whether in a museum, in a home, or on a mountaintop, time spent in gazing at an aesthetic good eventually loses its want-eliminating ability. The noblest enjoyments fall victim to the law of diminishing returns.

The law applies to human action. Excessive talk produces diminishing returns. A parent who repeats over and over the same commands to his or her children will have undisciplined children. Endless discipline is no discipline.

Life itself reflects diminishing returns. As population expands relative to space, life becomes increasingly cheap. Double or triple the population of the world dependent on a given volume of resources, and the value of people will fall just as the value of space will rise. People will die younger because the resources required for extending life will be more scarce; human character will change as poverty increases, suffering intensifies, and increasing crowds and congestion become more commonly accepted. Interdependences will change; friendships will become more withdrawn, punishments for infractions of order more severe. The number of people this planet can support is limited. As congestion intensifies, life approaches the anthill.

The law of diminishing returns combines with the law of economy to form the essential characteristics of the optimizing process. This process lends insight into an indefinitely large variety of business phenomena and has further applications outside the usual range of economic thinking.

The owner of a store, for example, is in the business of trading goods for money and money for inventories, hoping to make a profit on each turnover or at least on his total volume of sales. He buys a collection of goods (inventory) which he thinks his customers will eventually buy from him at higher prices. But his inventory costs money, since he either has to pay the bank interest on the money he has borrowed to finance the purchases or has to give up, if he is using his own money, the interest he could have earned by investing it in a savings account, a bond, or a share of stock. The store owner will be continually juggling his purchases as he learns what his customers want to buy from him, and he will not keep large inventories of items that will stand around for a long time. Because diminishing returns from particular items in his stocks would come into play, he will balance his purchases, spreading inventories over a wide selection of items. His income derives from profits, and he maximizes profits subject to the limitation imposed by the size of his resources, his capacity to manage his enterprise, and his borrowing power.

Banks are no exception to this optimizing process. They are in the business of providing credit. Individuals put their money into the bank for safekeeping, convenience, and the interest they can earn (if it is kept in a savings account). Banks lend money out to customers at interest, keeping a reserve, of course, and the difference between the interest they earn on loans and the interest they pay on deposits, after salaries and other expenses are paid, is the profit that can be distributed to the owners (shareholders) of the bank. Every day the bank manager is making more loans, every day customers are repaying loans. When the bank manager makes a loan, he is *buying promissory notes* from his borrowers, and the kind of notes he buys (which depends on the types of customers to whom he lends) have to be evaluated for riskiness, a factor that determines how much a particular bank is likely to lend to a particular customer. There is no difference in principle between the process of juggling sizes of loans to particular customers or choosing among borrowers and the process of deciding between ice cream or jelly beans in choosing a lunch.

Collective choosers, such as governments and other groups, are also continually engaged in the process of optimization. Governments provide public services to constituents—road, policy, defense, welfare—and the process of allocating a budget is a process of optimizing spending in each direction. Out of a specified quantity of tax income, plus permitted borrowing, expenditure is allocated to satisfy what the government representatives believe are the most urgent public needs. Because of the law of diminishing utility, not all of the tax money is spent on a space program, antimissile devices, roads, or welfare. Because of the same law, not all tax revenues are acquired from a single class or faction of taxpayers.

Some choosers may not appear to be adopting the optimizing principle. We may look around us and say that a certain person is not doing the thing for which he is best suited, that the government is putting too much money on this or that project, that a certain store isn't maximizing profits, and so on. But such observations merely reflect *our* judgment about what makes *other* people satisfied. There is no scientific way of proving that other people are making irrational choices.

Of course we may say this about ourselves. We may say we

are not optimizing agents because we do not know exactly what it is that constitutes the optimum. We live in a world of uncertainty and risk and do not even know how enjoyable we are going to find particular experiences. Trial and error help us to discover those things that help us to maximize profits, to increase our enjoyments, and to find a pleasing way of life. But as long as we think changes can be made for the better, we will in fact make those changes. If we did not, we would be masochists and have to include the love of unhappiness in our preferences!

The principle of optimization applies to all decision-making agents even though the decisions undertaken may not seem the most rational ones or, in the case of groups, command universal agreement. An artist (usually) does not make his painting all green, does not spatter hundreds of coats of paint on a single canvas, and does not make his painting a mile long; the law of diminishing returns alone would see to that. But given the combination of that law with the law of economy, he is even more selective, if not because of the cost of paint or the waste of his time, then because the intrusion of a single color, excessive size, or a lack of variety would destroy the effect he seeks to capture.

The principle of optimization is a fundamental principle of economics and a basic ingredient of all action. A composer of piano music maximizes the effect of a sequence of notes always subject to the "budget" constraint that the notes he inscribes are on the piano and that the sequence of notes is within the physical capacity of a pianist. Religious worship has its limits because of time constraints on the worshippers and competing duties or pleasures. Enjoyment of a museum is limited by the time available to the viewer. Beauty may have to be sacrificed in architecture when form conflicts with function. Passion too is confronted with biological "budget" limitations, and human activity is constrained by our "time budget," by the fact that in the long run, as individuals, we are dead.

4. *Price and Income Effects*

Rational choice, which implies optimization, means that expenditure patterns will be influenced by income and price. The pattern of expenditure will alter when prices or incomes are changed, and the resulting changes in demands and supplies are called price and income effects. We shall first consider the effects of changes in income at constant prices and then go on to consider the effects of changes in prices at constant real or money income.

Suppose a student decides to buy his lunch in a diner which serves hamburgers, milkshakes, coffee, pie, ice cream, and jelly beans. Hamburgers cost 40 cents, milkshakes are 30 cents, a cup of coffee is 10 cents, pie 20 cents, ice cream 10 cents, and jelly beans are ½ cent each. How will the student's choice of lunch be affected by changes in these prices?

Let us suppose first that he has lots of money, so that he does not need to ration his purchases on grounds of economy; he can buy as much as he wants of any item. The choice he will make will depend on his preferences, which of course will be affected by the law of diminishing returns. He will not, for example, have a lunch consisting entirely of jelly beans. His enjoyment will probably be greatest if he eats a rather balanced lunch.

His first impulse, let us suppose, is to buy two hamburgers, a piece of pie with ice cream, a milkshake, and a cup of coffee. Altogether he would pay $1.50 for this lunch.

After a bit of reflection, however, he decides this is excessive. Tastes, after all, are conditioned both by past experience and by anticipations about the future, and because of the latter he decides that his initial choice might help to make him fat; short-run considerations of taste have to give way to long-run well-being. Summoning up his Spartan instincts, therefore, he cuts out the ice cream on top of the pie. With no budget problems he would thus buy two hamburgers, a milkshake, a piece of pie, and a cup of coffee, costing a total of $1.40. This is his optimal choice when he has no budget constraint.

But now let us take a case where the student does not have lots of money. Suppose his income is reduced. Money he spends on lunch now is money that he cannot spend on other things—on supper, on lunch next day or next week, on clothes, on a movie, on his girl friend, on books, in paying for his education, or paying his taxes. He now has to be more economical. The alternative uses of money are so numerous that he will not ordinarily treat money as if it were a free good and spend it willy-nilly.

So he decides to reduce his luncheon expenditure to about $1 on the general principle that the saving will yield him the means to make other needed purchases. The reduction in his income thus has an *income effect* of 40 cents with respect to his luncheon expenditure.

For $1 he can get a hamburger, a milkshake, pie, and coffee; or he could get two hamburgers, ice cream, and coffee or some other combination. Suppose that he chooses two hamburgers, a dish of ice cream, and a cup of coffee. This choice is optimal, his best selection given existing prices and his now limited budget.

It is worth noticing, at this point, how the reduction in his total expenditure on lunch, due to his lower income, has affected his spending pattern. In the course of reducing his luncheon expediture by 40 cents he has eliminated the milkshake and the pie, continued to buy the hamburgers and the coffee, and added the ice cream. These expenditure changes are *income effects.* When income is lowered, there is a tendency to buy less of each good. But this is not a general law. When income goes down, it is quite possible for consumption of some goods to go up, and when income goes up, consumption of some goods may go down.

Because of this possibility goods can be divided into three classes. First there are goods of which more is bought as income increases; these goods are called *superior goods* (or, often, simply goods). Then there are goods of which less is bought as income increases; these are called *inferior goods.* Goods which are on the borderline—goods whose consumption remains constant over the range of variation of income we are considering—are called *neutral goods.*

Whether a good is inferior, neutral, or superior in the consumption of a particular individual depends on the types of satisfactions—attributes—the good can provide to the individual. The cheapest Chevrolet, Ford, or Volkswagen can provide transportation—if it runs—but more expensive cars may also provide more comfort, greater reliability, and a certain snob value.* Insofar as consumers are willing to spend more for comfort, reliability, and prestige as their incomes rise, cars providing these attributes are superior goods, and those that do not are inferior or neutral goods.

In the examples of the student's choice of lunch, the reduction in the student's income induced him to eliminate the milkshake and pie from his lunch and to add ice cream. Thus over this range of the student's budget ice cream is an inferior good, hamburgers and coffee are neutral goods, and milkshakes and pie are superior goods. We shall see that these distinctions play an important role in the theory of price.

* Snob-value, or prestige, effects are often called Veblenesque effects in honor of the economist and social critic Thorstein Veblen, who analyzed the interdependence of individual expenditure patterns in particular social classes.

To show the reactions of the student to price changes, suppose there is a change in the price of a hamburger. The change in the demand for hamburger is called the *price effect*. Suppose it goes up to 50 cents. Assuming that preferences were unchanged (and preferences, or tastes, *in contrast to choices*, are not directly affected by prices), how would this price change affect his choice of lunch?

The first thing to notice about the increase in price is that it makes the purchaser worse off. It reduces his opportunities. His money income is the same, but the price of one of the goods he buys has gone up, and this reduces the purchasing power of his given income. Only if he were given an extra 20 cents in income would he be able to buy the same things he could have bought before the price went up.

The fact that the increase in price lowers the student's real income means that the price change will affect demand solely on account of the fact that he is worse off. There is, in other words, an income effect implicit within any price change. The reduction in his *real* (the purchasing power of his money income) income means he will have to buy less of some things.

But the income effect is not the whole story. A price change contains both an *income effect* and a *substitution effect*. Even if the price change had no income effect at all, there would be a tendency for the pattern of purchases to change just because of the substitution effect. On account of the substitution effect our student will tend to rearrange his purchase in such a way as to economize on the good that has gone up in price, substituting other goods for it.

Let us see the effect of the increase in the price of hamburgers. If the student still buys two hamburgers, he will have to give up both the ice cream and the coffee. Let us suppose he refuses to give up his coffee. One solution would be for him to buy one hamburger, a milkshake, ice cream, and coffee, in effect substituting a milkshake for the hamburger he could have bought before the price went up. This may be his new optimal lunch, given his constraints, but it cannot give the same satisfaction as the original selection. After all, he could have chosen this lunch before, but he did not do so; his preferences for the original combination have already been revealed.

Is there a law of price change implicit in this example? The answer is yes, but the law is not what it would seem to be. You cannot say that if the price of a good goes up, less of it will be bought; you can only say that if the price of a good goes up *and real income remains the same,* less of the good will be bought. The substitution effect per se always means that at a higher price a smaller quantity will be bought, but it is conceivable that the substitution effect can be offset or more than offset by an income effect working in the opposite direction.

Consider our example again in order to see why the substitution effect is always negative. Before the price of hamburgers went up, the student could buy two hamburgers, ice cream, and coffee for $1. After the price change the same lunch would cost him $1.20. If we now give him 20 cents more to spend on lunch, just as an experiment, to abstract from the income effect, he can buy the same lunch as before the price change. But he is slightly better off than before, because even with the higher price of hamburgers, he has alternatives available to him not open before; in other words, the extra 20 cents overcompensates him somewhat for the price change. He could buy, for example, one hamburger, a milkshake, ice cream, and coffee while keeping 20 cents in his pocket for use another day; or he could buy one hamburger, two milkshakes, and a cup of coffee; or one hamburger, two dishes of ice cream, and a cup of coffee and have 40 cents left over. If we abstract from the income effect, an increase in price always induces a smaller demand.

To take an even more clear-cut case but one that is in principle the same, suppose you have decided to buy a car the price of which is $2,000, but just before you have a chance to buy it, the price goes up to $4,000. At this higher price you cannot afford the car; the purchasing power of your income has gone down.

But now suppose that someone compensates you for the increase in the price of the car by giving you an extra $2,000. You are now able to buy the car, and if you do so, you will be in the same position as if the price had not risen. But in fact you will probably decide not to buy this car at the price of $4,000. You are likely to spend the extra $2,000 on other things —taxi rides, clothes, a trip to Honolulu, and so on—or to buy a competing brand of car the price of which has not risen or has gone up by less. This is the essence of the substitution effect, the fact that even though your real income is not lower than before, you tend to shift purchases from goods which have risen in price.

Thus we see that the price effect is composed of a substitution effect and an income effect. The substitution effect alone, that is, the effect on purchases abstracting from the change in real income it produces, always works to reduce purchases of a product whose price has risen; on this account an increase in price reduces demand. But the income effect may work in another direction. An increase in the price of a product that a man *consumes* always reduces real income, but the income change may raise or lower the amount bought. Normally, of course, people buy more of a good as their income increases. But the normal case is not the only case, since we have to allow for the possibility of inferior goods—goods which at low incomes consumers buy a lot of, but which at higher incomes they do without.

Because goods may be inferior, it cannot be asserted as a general proposition that an increase in price will cause a reduction in quantity bought, although it remains true that the substitution effect alone, abstracting from the change in real income induced by it, does cause a reduction in quantity purchased when the price goes up.

These propositions are perfectly general. A consumer who finds the price of a product he buys rising will substitute other goods for it in the process of *reoptimization* unless income effects are negative and dominate the substitution effect. A business that faces a rising price of labor will try to substitute machines for labor if it is at all possible. A bank that finds the interest rate it has to pay on savings accounts rising may try to attract checking-account customers by offering better facilities for checking services. A university that finds the price of professors in one field of scientific research rising may try to specialize in other fields. A local government that finds the cost of providing a given standard of welfare to the needy rising may try to provide welfare services in other forms. The national government that is confronted with rising costs of one defense implement may substitute others for it. In all these examples one can see the generality of the principle of substitution. As prices change, a continual juggling at the margin of choice is made to achieve an optimum pattern of purchases.

The income effect can play tricks, especially when we deal with different types of consumers. Consider an increase in air pollution in a large city. This lowers real income in the aggregate because it reduces current comfort and life expectancy with no compensating benefits. Thus you would expect that the price effect would drive people from the polluted cities toward cities with clean air. This would certainly be true if everybody's real income were the same after as before the pollution; the substitution effect alone would drive people away.

But the income effect applied to aggregates may have an opposite result. One class in the population, let us say the rich, may have a greater aversion to dirty air than do the poor.

There are two reasons why this may be so. First, clean air in industrial countries is a luxury that is more highly prized after more urgent wants are taken care of; second, pollution is a cumulative process that reduces life expectancy, which increases the cost of pollution more to the rich than to the poor because the life expectancy of the rich is higher, on the average. (Whether this is statistically true or not, let us assume it is for the sake of argument.)

As a result of the increase in pollution the rich move away, lowering rents and property values in low-density housing areas they occupy; and the lower rents may attract the poorer classes, who split up existing dwellings and turn the vacated areas formerly inhabited by the rich into high-density dwelling areas. Property values per lot may rise, but rents per family will fall; and since rents constitute a relatively large proportion of the budget of the poor, the poor may be attracted to the city and, indeed, be made better off as a consequence of the pollution! If the process were carried far enough, the poor would become concentrated in the polluted cities and the rich in unpolluted cities. Thus an increase in pollution in a city can result in a higher rather than a lower population.

To summarize: A change in the price of a good affects the demand for it by an amount which is called the *price effect*. The price effect can be divided into an *income effect* and a *substitution effect*. On account of the substitution effect alone, less of the good will be bought at higher prices; the principle of substitution always works against purchases of the goods whose price has risen. Normally, the substitution effect will be reinforced by the income effect since at higher prices a purchaser is worse off and consumers buy less of most things at lower incomes. But this is not the only possible case, since some goods can be inferior. The law of price has to take into account the possibility of inferior goods. The safe generalization, which is the law of price, is that *more of a good is bought as its price falls if more of a good is bought as income rises.*

5. *Cash, Liquidity, and Stock Management*

Economic man is schizophrenic, his split personality emerging both as producer and consumer. As a producer he makes and sells goods, a process which requires effort; as a consumer he buys and absorbs goods, a process which increases enjoyment.

In his role as producer-consumer the individual has to coordinate his plans for producing and selling with his plans for buying and consuming. An excess of buying over selling implies an excess of paying over receiving and therefore a reduction in cash holdings; and an excess of selling over buying implies an excess of receiving over paying and therefore an increase in cash holdings. An individual chooser will generally know exactly which receipts and payments are being made at a particular time. But more complex organizational units, including families, firms, banks, governments, and nations, cannot so easily coordinate plans for selling and buying, and this gives rise to the possibility of discrepancies between receipts and payments that can cause considerable fluctuations in cash holdings.

Let us begin with the financial plans of a rather general unit; for the sake of simplicity, we shall take a family. Let us imagine a division of labor within the family with the husband doing the selling and the wife the buying. Every day the man goes out to the market to sell his services, depositing the sales proceeds in the family till in the evening; every day the woman goes out to the market to buy, taking cash with her from the family till to pay for cash transactions during the day.

A balance of cash will usually be retained in the till over and above the needs for a day's shopping to allow for contingencies of one kind or another—sickness, unemployment, a fall in wages, an increase in the price of one of the wife's regular purchases, the need to have cash to take advantage of an unexpected opportunity. These contingencies are worth preparing oneself for, and provide one of the motives for holding cash over and above daily requirements. The extent of the need and willingness to hold a cash reserve, and therefore its magnitude, will be based on the size of everyday purchases, the risk of emergencies, and the likelihood of speculative opportunities. The amount of cash on hand may on the average be a given proportion of income or so many days' or weeks' expenses. Whatever the amount of cash, the preference for cash is based on the need for one of its services, *liquidity*. Liquid assets are assets that are easily convertible into other assets, and cash is generally the most liquid of all assets.

We can see the usefulness of cash now as a means of bridging any gaps between the daily stream of receipts of the husband and the daily stream of purchases of the wife. When purchases exceed receipts, the cash balance goes down; when receipts exceed purchases, the cash balance goes up. An excess of expenditures over family income is a gap between outpayments and inpayments, and we say that the family has a (balance-of-payments) *surplus* when receipts exceed payments and the cash balance is going up, a *deficit* when payments exceed receipts and the cash balance is going down; we say that the family is in a position of *equilibrium* when receipts equal payments and there is no change (and no desire for a change) in the cash balance.

Receipts on a given day are not, of course, likely to equal payments on that day. The purpose of holding cash reserves is precisely so that you can use the cash reserves you have on hand to make transactions in excess of income as the need arises, to take advantage of a good opportunity, or to tide you over an emergency. But on the average over a period of time receipts cannot fall very much short of payments. If they did, a liquidity problem would develop; the family would face the prospect of running out of cash.

The cost of a liquidity shortage can be very high indeed. If you have to balance receipts and payments too closely, you may have to pass up good bargains, borrow at expensive interest rates to pay emergency hospital bills, or fail to meet educational needs or pay your taxes. Some irregularities in the stream of payments and receipts are inevitable, and you should keep some excess cash on hand or in the bank to avoid the necessity for making costly sudden adjustments.

There is a certain unevenness in spending and earning patterns. The husband may be paid for his services only once every week, fortnight, or month. Typically the husband will deposit his salary in the bank every month, while the wife will go about the business of shopping every day or perhaps once a week. In this case the cash balance will be high at the beginning of the month and gradually fall toward zero (or the minimum extra cash balance the family tries to hold) toward the end of the month. Discipline is required at the beginning of the month, since it would be most unwise for the wife to spend a whole month's income on rent, groceries, and other needs in the first two weeks. If this discipline is not present the family will suffer from a liquidity crisis toward the end of the month. Experience (or intrafamily strife) will teach the wife the expenditure pattern over time that is feasible with a given income, or the husband the income that is needed to maintain a given expenditure.

The problem of adjusting expenditure to income and avoiding the liquidity shortage to which failure to adjust gives rise is not limited to the individual or family. A business firm typically is selling goods from its stocks and buying goods and labor services and raw materials to replenish its stocks every day.

A firm must remain liquid if it is to meet its bills and be able to take advantage of profitable opportunities, and it cannot for long pay out more than it takes in without running out of cash and going bankrupt.

A bank is continually making new loans and receiving repayments and interest on old loans. The difference between its receipts and payments, after taking account of salaries, dividends, and other expenses, is its *balance of payments.* The bank's reserves go down when receipts fall short of payments and up when receipts exceed payments. But since a bank must always be able to meet depositors' checks, keeping its deposits convertible into legal tender, it must be sure to keep an adequate cash reserve. It may indeed be required by law to keep additional cash reserves in the national central bank, as part of the government regulations that banks in most countries are subject to. The cost of a bank becoming illiquid is especially serious because it cannot afford to lose the confidence of its depositors in its ability to convert bank deposits into ready cash. In most advanced countries, of course, there are ready markets for day-to-day loans, so that banks can readily borrow excess reserves from one another.*

The government budget is another case in point. Taxes accrue as receipts to the government at special times during the year, while government payments for defense, welfare, roads, and other services are made throughout the course of the year. The government keeps a cash balance available to tide over any gap between tax receipts and government expenditures, and if it gets into a particularly tight cash position, it may find itself in the embarrassing position of having to ask an unwilling

* In the United States this market is the Federal funds market in which commercial banks lend their excess reserves to one another. The so-called Euro-dollar market (more correctly the international short-term credit market) performs a somewhat analogous function in European money markets. It is a market to which central and commercial banks have at least indirect access.

Congress for permission to borrow money to pay its bills and for an extension of the public debt limit. Perhaps more typically the government will issue short-term debts (treasury bills) to borrow money while awaiting tax payments, and corporations and large taxpayers awaiting liabilities will invest their cash temporarily in treasury bills or similar instruments.

The national balance of payments is another application of the same need to preserve an adequate cash balance. Most countries keep their currencies convertible into another major currency or into gold. The United States, whose currency is at the center of the world's monetary system, keeps the dollar convertible into gold for the monetary purposes of foreign central banks. If the United States spends (or lends) more than it buys (or borrows) from foreign countries, other countries acquire dollars they may not want to hold; if so, they can exchange them for gold in the United States, causing a reduction in the United States gold stock.* If the country as a whole keeps on spending more than it is earning, the loss of gold could bring on a liquidity crisis. For this reason every country has to make sure that it maintains a sound liquidity position; of course, countries sometimes have difficulties (like everybody else) in doing so. We will go into this in much greater detail in later chapters.

I have used the term "liquidity" up until now as if it applied only to cash holdings. But it should be clear now that economic concepts have application outside the realm of what are narrowly considered economic transactions. The concept of liquidity in its widest interpretation does not apply only to money and cash transactions. It can be applied to any scarce resource at all. An individual who takes on too many commitments on his time can face a liquidity problem with respect to time. You have often seen people who are doing an excessive number of

* In this case gold is moved from Fort Knox to the Federal Reserve Bank of New York, where foreign central bankers have gold in safekeeping. The gold thus moved is called earmarked gold.

things and have no time to spare for many urgent commitments. They have a *temporal* liquidity problem (an extreme shortage of time) and may pay a huge penalty for it in the form of not being able to produce products of usual quality, perform services up to standard, or allocate leisure and enjoyment properly. An excessively busy man is a man who has let himself run out of the leisure needed to make efficient choices. It takes time to optimize on ordinary transactions, and an excessively busy man—like a harassed secretary—can no longer optimize.

One can think of several other examples of temporal liquidity problems. The professional chess player can let himself get into a position of time shortage if he delays too long on a few moves. A professor may commit himself to so many things that he fails to perform urgent duties. A businessman may undertake so many business arrangements that he has no time for mental improvement or physical exercise. A college student may commit himself to so many courses that he cannot perform any of them adequately, or may spend so much time with friends that he has no time for studies.

Businesses that keep insufficient inventories run into bottlenecks, a manifestation of a lack of liquidity in the sphere of inventories. Other examples include households that do not keep extra fuses or candles in the event of light failure; cars that possess an insufficient reserve of gasoline; Cabinet members who so preoccupy themselves with detailed decisions or diversions that they have no mental reserve left over to cope with big problems when they arise; generals who occupy themselves so much with tactical considerations that they lose track of strategy, and northern cities like Chicago that do not keep a sufficient reserve of snowplows on hand.

These examples are all manifestations of liquidity problems arising from the failure to provide a proper balance between receipts and expenditures—of money, time, or goods.

The cost of running out of cash (or indeed any asset) may be high as just suggested. What, then, is it that prevents individuals and groups from holding large stocks of assets they might need in the event of emergencies? Why do not individuals hold huge cash balances and keep large stocks of every imaginable asset that could be useful in emergencies? Why does Chicago not buy enough snowplows to meet the heaviest snowfalls?

The answer, of course, is the same as the answer to any economic question. There are, it is true, gains in holding liquid assets, but there are also costs. The extra gain—the *marginal benefit*—from holding additional quantities of any asset decreases with the quantity of the asset held. No one can insure against all risks and insurance costs money.

When an individual (or group) holds cash, he acquires the liquidity convenience of the cash but foregoes the income that could be earned by investing it in earning assets. Money kept in a sock or in a checking account is money not put into a savings account which earns interest or into a bond or share of stock or commodity. The cost of holding money idle is therefore the profit or interest yield given up by not investing it (after taking into account any transactions costs involved). This means that the higher the rate of interest a person would be able to earn by putting money into alternative assets, the smaller the quantity of money he would want to hold.

In periods of inflation, when the money price of commodities is rising, the cost of holding money increases. As the price of commodities goes up, money depreciates; its purchasing power falls. On this account, while people may try to hold a larger nominal quantity of dollars, they will certainly want to hold a smaller real quantity, that is, a smaller value in terms of purchasing power over commodities. People will economize on their cash balances.

In times of deflation, when the money price of goods is going down, the opposite happens. The cost of holding money goes down correspondingly. Money appreciates, and individuals are encouraged to hold larger real cash balances, that is, a greater value in terms of purchasing power over goods. People economize on other things whose dollar prices are going down as they shift out of goods into money.

But the real responsiveness of cash balances to changes in the cost of holding cash is not different from the responsiveness of holding any asset idle when the cost of holding it changes. Housewives hold stocks of groceries available for emergencies and convenience, but would economize on their holdings if the price of the groceries were expected to fall or the advantages of using the money in other ways increased. Similar examples include wine stored in the wine cellar, free time available for use as the need arises, stocks of spare parts held by firms, and holdings of excess reserves by banks.

The problem of determining which assets to keep idle, in reserve, and which to use in exchange is one of the most important problems of choice in economics. On the one hand, it is nice to keep reserves on hand of a lot of assets that might prove useful in an emergency. On the other hand, an overcommitment of resources to the luxury of keeping stocks of all potentially useful assets, whether money, time, or goods, exacts a continuing cost, a duplication of effort, and a waste of resources. It is wasteful to be too liquid; it is costly to be too illiquid. A balancing of the benefits and costs is necessary.

6. *Money and Gold*

The best way to understand the many functions money serves is to imagine the principal inconveniences that would be experienced in its absence. First of all, in the absence of money there would be no uniform *standard of measure,* or *unit of account.* If a rancher had only steers to sell and wanted to buy a car or the services of a plumber, it would be very hard to ascertain how many hours of plumbing services he ought to obtain for a steer or how many steers he ought to pay for a car. Also, each calculation would have to be repeated for each transaction, and the total cost of making transactions would increase sharply with the number of commodities involved. Suppose, to take another case, that there is no money and there are only two commodities, salt and wheat; then there is only one calculation (the price of salt in terms of wheat or, as in all cases, its reciprocal, the price of wheat in terms of salt). If we add a third commodity, say, butter, we then have three calculations (the price of salt in terms of wheat, the price of butter in terms of wheat, and the price of butter in terms of salt); if we add a fourth commodity, say, theater tickets, we have six calculations, having to add the price of theater tickets in terms of each of the other commodities; if we add a fifth commodity, we have four more calculations. Each time we add a commodity, we add as many more calculations as there were previous commodities. If n is the initial number of commodities, the addition of another commodity increases the number of calculations by $n - 1$. The formula relating the number of calculations T to the number of commodities is then

$T = \frac{1}{2}n(n-1)$, as you can see for yourself if you try it out on the examples I have given.

The labor in these calculations becomes enormous as the number of commodities increases. Thus if we have 1,000 commodities, there would have to be $T = \frac{1}{2} \times 1{,}000\,(1{,}000 - 1) = 499{,}500$ calculations, a very large and therefore expensive number of calculations to make; you can imagine the work involved in this modern age with its millions of commodities and hundreds of millions of people. Suppose, for example, that each person makes 1,000 transactions per month (about thirty-five a day). This would mean $12 \times 499{,}500 = 5{,}994{,}000$ calculations per person per year. And setting the active (transacting) population of the world at 2 billion, this would mean 11,988,000,000,000,000 calculations per year! I leave it for you to determine that on the assumption that each calculation involved a wastage of time worth only 0.01 cent per calculation, the total cost would be over $1 trillion—more than the entire gross national product of the United States.

A first function of money is to avoid such unnecessary calculations. Just as it is convenient to adopt common measures of length (inches, feet, yards), so it is an enormous aid to calculation to adopt a common language in which to express value. In no other way can values be arranged on a scale, and in no other way can an individual easily calculate the value of his possessions.

So great are the conveniences of a single measure of value that if dollars and cents performed no other function and so did not exist, they, or something else like them, would have to be created for this purpose. As this suggests, the common measure of value need not be dollars at all. We could calculate everything in terms of the number of bushels of wheat or fractions of bushels of wheat that have to be given up to buy commodities; or we could calculate everything in terms of gold, platinum, or anything under the sun. The gain from a common measure could be had even if the common measure expressed no real thing at all. We could calculate everything in terms of a unit of account like shekels, the old Biblical currency, or in terms of guineas (which are still used as a unit of quotation in England even though they no longer exist as currency) or any artificial contrivance at all. The fact is, however, that while there are examples of artificial contrivances used as units of account, dollars are used in the United States, pounds in England, francs in France, and so on, because the (enormously important) unit-of-account function is closely related to the many other functions money performs, and there are advantages in concentrating all these functions in a single thing.

The second great advantage of money is that it serves as a *unit of contract.* When you are fitted for a coat at a store, when you place an order with one of the department-store chains for home delivery, or when you make any purchase at all without paying cash for it, you are quoted a price in dollars (if you live in the United States) because money serves as a unit of account, the first function of money described; but you also *agree to pay* the dollar amount quoted. In this sense money is serving as a unit of contract as well as a measure in which values are expressed.

A unit of contract is especially important for agreements made over time. If you borrow money to buy a house, the terms of your mortgage will be expressed in dollars, and you will be committed to pay a sum of money every month for the duration of your mortgage contract. In principle you could agree to pay instead so much bread or provide so many hours of your services, but in fact your debt will be expressed in terms of dollars (or the currency of whatever country you live in), and dollars are what you will commit yourself to pay.

The advantages of a single unit of contract instead of many are so great that its absence can hardly be imagined. The future is to ordinary mortals uncertain, and it cannot be expected that every person can make even a roughly accurate estimate of the prices to be assumed by individual commodities in the future. If you were committed to pay your mortgage debt in some combination of automobiles, wheat, and clothes, for example, you would have to form an estimate of the exchange value of each of these goods in the future. If all your debts and assets are expressed in terms of dollars, you need only form an estimate of the value of one thing, dollars, in the future. You need only form an estimate of general tendencies toward changes in the purchasing power of money.

The uses of money as a unit of account and as a unit of contract are so important that if money served no other purpose, it would have to be recognized as one of the great inventions of mankind. But we have not yet come to the most important function of money, the one which allows an extension of the division of labor and the increased income that results from specialization. It is money in its role of *medium of exchange* which enables such specialization to exist and without which the great modern economies could not function.

Imagine the inconvenience of dispensing with money as a medium of exchange. A plumber going to a shop to get his shoes repaired would have to pay the shoemaker in a good the shoemaker wanted to consume, but if the shoemaker did not want exactly the quantity of plumbing services that would exchange for the shoe repairs, the plumber would have to sell his plumbing services to someone who had the goods the shoemaker wanted and transport them to the shoemaker. A farmer with a cow to sell who wanted to buy a ticket to see a performance of *Aïda* at the Metropolitan would find it extremely difficult to bring his cow to the box office and hope to get his proper change.

It is to avoid such inconveniences and embarrassments that money, as a medium of exchange, would have to be created if it did not already exist. If there were no medium of exchange, one would quickly develop. Every person would hasten to exchange some of the commodities he had for others which, though not needed for the satisfaction of immediate wants, were themselves readily exchangeable for those he needed. Out of this process one or more of the commodities would naturally develop as a medium of exchange increasingly used in ever-increasing circles of commerce. Commodities suitable for this purpose would have to be desirable, divisible, storable, and portable and would have to retain their value better than most commodities. But I am describing an actual historical process. Because of their natural efficiency, gold and silver were settled upon in very early times, through custom, convenience, and tacit concurrence, as common mediums of exchange, and it was only natural that they took on the properties of money in its role of unit of contract and unit of account as well. For centuries these commodities have served as a store of value and performed as well the other functions of money, for which they were well adapted because of their divisibility, indestructibility, homogeneity, portability, stability of value, and indeed beauty. These advantages of gold and silver are so great that although guns, cigarettes, wampum, cowrie shells, iron, ivory tusks, rock salt, and a vast number of other commodities have been used at one time or another as a unit of account, gold and silver have been most lasting. Because of their natural advantages as money within nations, it was only natural that they became the unit in which exchanges between nations were transacted.

Gold and silver became solidly entrenched as money in the modern era. But among the great inventions of recent times was the development of bank credit as a substitute for gold and silver. Bank credit performed the various functions of money even better and cheaper than did gold and silver themselves. Despite their advantages, gold and silver suffered from the erosion of hand-to-hand circulation, the risk of robbery when carried on the person, and physical encumbrance for large, transactions. This was especially true with gold which was typically between 10 and 20 times as valuable (per ounce) as silver. It became customary, therefore, for large gold hoards to be deposited for safekeeping, sometimes with goldsmiths but often with rich merchants whose credit and honesty were beyond dispute. Stocks of gold were locked up in merchants' vaults, and the possession of such stocks enabled them to lend money out at interest. However, money was often lent out, not in the form of gold, but in the form of claims on gold, payable on demand by the merchant. These claims began to circulate as a means of payment, and they served this function perfectly well as long as trust in the merchant houses—trust in their ability to convert claims into gold—remained. The process was so successful that it soon turned out to be unnecessary to keep an ounce of gold as backing against every claim on an ounce of gold in the merchant house, since as long as trust in the merchant house existed, not all claims would be presented at once. Thus the merchant house became a bank, and the banker became a specialist in seeking out good investments for the excess gold—that quantity he held over and above the amount needed to preserve confidence in convertibility. This meant that the banker specialized in seeking out good credit risks—usually other merchants with profitable projects to finance and able and willing to pay interest. Banking thus became a profitable enterprise, and competition among banks for deposits of gold led to great extensions of the means of payment: a given value of gold served as the reserve base behind bank credit, which began to replace gold as the most important means of payment. Bank credit, however, had to be convertible into gold (or silver), and any banker who allowed his customers to doubt his reputation for ready conversion of deposits into gold would quickly face withdrawals and go bankrupt. The soundness of a bank and the reputation of the banker became closely identified.

Thus gold, which in early times had been itself the predominant means of payment, became the reserve behind a more important means of payment—bank deposits—between the seventeenth and the early part of the twentieth century. The process became extended still further as dominant *national* (central) banks arose. Private bankers began to keep their own reserves, not in gold, but in deposits at the central bank, and gold, which formerly circulated as coin for hand-to-hand transactions, was gradually replaced by bank notes of the central bank. In nearly every country the central bank became the custodian of the nation's gold reserve, which was used, up until 1914, as backing behind the notes (cash) issued by the central bank. Commercial banks had to keep their deposits convertible into central bank notes, and the central banker had to keep his notes (and deposits) convertible into gold. The gold standard thus started off with pure gold (specie) but turned into a gold-reserve standard with money encompassing not only gold but also all those things convertible into gold. As long as confidence in the convertibility of bank deposits into central bank notes and of central bank notes into gold persisted, no one believed it necessary actually to make the conversion.

The First World War changed all that. In 1914 most central banks, including the Bank of England (which occupied a special position as the nucleus of the international gold standard), suspended the convertibility of their notes into gold, and the gold standard outside the United States broke down. Attempts to restore it in the 1920s failed miserably when the Bank of England set a gold value on the pound sterling that was too high, the Bank of France a gold value on the franc which was too low, and the United States departed from the principles of the gold standard that had been developed in the course of the preceding century.* Gold rushed to France and to the United States, and by 1931, in the midst of the Depression, the Bank of England decided it had to suspend convertibility again. By the time a chance for restoration of the system had appeared in

* I shall go into these matters in detail in later chapters.

1934, after the United States raised the price of gold to its current level of $35 an ounce, the spread of totalitarianism in Italy, Spain, Germany, Russia, and Eastern Europe had destroyed the possibility of a restoration of international political harmony, without which the gold standard—or any system of international economic order, for that matter—cannot operate.

After the Second World War a modified gold-standard system was set up under the United Nations agreements at Bretton Woods, New Hampshire, that created the International Monetary Fund (IMF). By this time the dollar had emerged as a world currency, and American gold policy determined the reserve base of the system. Central bankers, instead of holding only gold in their reserves, held dollars which, for the monetary purposes of foreign central banks, were convertible into gold at the United States Treasury. Only after 1958, after the creation of the Common Market and the restoration of currency convertibility in Europe, did gold come back into its own.

7. *Investment and Time*

Let us now go back to consider individual decisions in a different context. We have seen how individuals, families, and groups, in the process of producing and consuming, finance gaps between purchases and sales by drawing on, or adding to, cash reserves. They do this while taking into account the need to preserve an extra cash balance in the pocket, at home, or in the bank as a reserve for contingencies and as a *masse de manoeuvre* in the event a speculative opportunity arises. This basic liquidity decision is made in the context of general choice in which the husband-producer-seller optimizes by producing and selling those goods and services that cost the least, and the wife-buyer-consumer optimizes by buying those goods and services yielding the most satisfaction for the collective consumption of the family, for a minimum cost.

There is another dimension of choice that overlaps with the liquidity decisions just discussed, and that additional dimension is the subject of the present chapter. Each chooser has to divide expenditure in some proportion between present and future consumption. The part of income that is not consumed is, of course, *savings;* resources devoted to expanding future income are *investment.* The allocation of present resources to future consumption is the essence of investment.

Just as monthly salaries are not spent in a day, so daily purchases are not consumed in a day. Even purchases of commodities like bread, cheese, and wine and other foods that are enjoyed as they are consumed may yet be stored at home for a time. The act of purchasing is thus separate from the act of consuming. A washing machine, a television set, a car, a painting, a case of Scotch, a house—these are goods which are not consumed immediately upon acquisition, but instead yield a flow of benefits—*use value*—for months or years in the future. And there is a third category of purchases—stocks, bonds, insurance, and other financial assets that do not yield any *direct* enjoyment at all except the sense of security due to the fact that they are *claims* to receipts that will accrue in the future, enhancing the possibility of enjoyment at a later date.

The essential characteristic of investment is the dominant role played by time. Purchases made today may yield enjoyment or income in the future; sales made today may reduce enjoyment or receipts in the future. Optimal choice thus becomes dynamical. Dynamic optimization involves the process of selecting patterns of benefits and costs at different periods of time.

Let us go back to the husband-wife partnership. After marriage the bridegroom goes out to work, earning a salary, let us suppose, that is sufficient to maintain the couple on a modest standard of living. The husband's earnings are put in the bank, and the bride writes checks on them to finance daily purchases for food, transportation, clothing, and amusements and to pay periodic bills for rent, utilities, and so on.

Suppose the salary earnings are high enough to more than cover ordinary everyday expenses, and the couple find that their balance in the bank rises over time; they develop a balance-of-payments surplus. Their liquidity mounts until they have more than enough to meet ordinary contingencies.

As we saw in Chapter 5, it is "costly" to accumulate unnecessary cash balances, since cash yields no pecuniary return. A dollar in a checking account (or in a sock) is worth only a dollar one year hence. The first step, therefore, in the couple's saving plan is to transfer some of the idle funds to a savings account to take advantage of the interest that can be earned on it. This account is less liquid than a checking account because checks cannot be written on it,* but it is still highly liquid, since all it takes is a trip to the bank to withdraw cash or transfer money from a savings account to a checking account. At the same time the money in a savings account yields interest while it is idle; thus $100 put in a savings account today will accumulate to $104 next year if the interest rate on savings accounts is 4 percent. Savings accounts are the ideal place for a family to keep its contingency reserve and *masse de manoeuvre* because the assets are liquid enough and yet earn some interest.

Soon, however, the extra savings pile up in the savings account, and since money in a savings account also adds to liquidity while it does not yield a high rate of return, the couple become needlessly liquid. They then decide to look for more lucrative places to invest their money.

Concurrent with this accumulation of cash, the couple have presumably been adding to the refinement and comforts of the home by purchasing durable consumer goods—furniture, a television set, a car, and so on. The purchase of such durable goods is a consumer asset yielding enjoyments over time for which a lump sum of money is paid today. They may have borrowed in order to finance these purchases. They may, for example, have bought on credit. In this case they will have bought a stream of future enjoyments (enjoyments from the continuing use of the assets they have bought) and committed themselves to a stream of future costs (interest payments and repayment of the debt). Optimization implies that the gains from the stream of benefits provided by the good are com-

* This refers to United States practice, in which the bankers are not permitted to pay interest on demand deposits and the customers are not permitted to write checks on time deposits. Economic theory has long ago demonstrated that these prohibitions are neither necessary conditions of sound banking nor optimal arrangements from the standpoint of efficiency. Despite the long-standing history of the regulation, understanding on these matters is growing in the United States, and prospects for reform are hopeful.

mensurate with the stream of costs connected with repaying the loan, including the interest charges implicit in it.

If the couple have been accumulating excess cash in the bank, it is unlikely that they will have resorted to very much borrowing or credit buying. But if they do have excess cash and are in debt, they will first see whether or not it is worth paying off their debts. To check this, they need to look at the interest rate they pay on their credit purchases. If it happens to be less than what they are earning on their savings account (it won't be!), there would be no point in paying off their debts; indeed, this would result in net losses. But in fact they will find that the interest rates they are paying for the credit purchases of their television set, furniture, and car are probably over 10 percent when all the charges are taken into account—very much higher than the interest rate on their savings balance. By taking money out of their savings account and using it to repay their debts, they may be sacrificing interest at the rate of 4 percent and in effect getting instead an interest rate of more than 10 percent. They should do this as rapidly as is consistent with the preservation of their liquidity position.

An exception, however, will be their house, if they decide to buy one. A house is a *very* durable good. Whereas a typical household utility like a washing machine lasts, on the average, about eight years, a house may last thirty or fifty years, depending on its age and quality. For this reason there is a separate market for financing houses, a *mortgage market.*

A bank or a savings and loan association can lend money on the security of this very durable (and marketable) asset at good terms—perhaps as low as 5 or 6 percent. This is getting very close to the rate of interest the couple get on their savings account in the bank. If they have decided to buy a house and have taken out a 6 percent mortgage, they may prefer to keep some money in the savings account at 4 percent rather than pay off the mortgage, because the extra liquidity provided by the savings account now costs them only an extra 2 percent. Besides, the interest they pay on this mortgage in the United States (though not in most other countries) is tax-deductible, so that the interest cost of the mortgage is even lower than it appears. (The importance of this factor will depend on which tax bracket they are in.)

In deciding whether to buy a house or rent one, the couple will have had to compare the rental they would have to pay to rent a house with the depreciation, interest, and property-tax charges on houses they could buy. In buying a house, they would make a down payment from their own savings and then arrange for monthly payments of interest and repayment of principal (amortization) involved. Taking into account the amounts of all these as well as the expected resale value of their house at the time they are likely to sell it, they will calculate whether they are better off renting or buying.

Expectations about the price of the house in the future will be influenced by expectations about the future of the neighborhood in which the house is located, about likely innovations in construction techniques that would affect the price of competing new houses, and about the likelihood of changes in the purchasing power of money. For example, if all prices, wages, and rent rose because of general inflation, the price of the house, on this account alone, would go up along with other prices, while the monthly interest payments would stay constant in dollar terms, making purchase a very good investment indeed as compared to rental. Of course if the interest rate were correspondingly higher because of the inflation (and it usually is if everybody expects inflation, because lenders demand a premium to compensate for the depreciation of money), this factor could cancel at least part of the benefits.

The bond and stock markets are alternative outlets for surplus funds that might go into a house. The couple, after providing for immediate needs, liquidity, and some durable assets, may hope for more lucrative returns by purchasing bonds or stocks. A bond is a claim to a stream of future receipts fixed in terms of dollars. For a one-year bond you pay a sum of money, say \$100, and get back \$100 at the end of a year plus interest worth \$5 if the interest rate is 5 percent. Next year you could invest both the principal and the interest, \$105, on which you might again get 5 percent interest yielding $\$105 \times 0.05 = \$5.25$.

This means that if you invested \$100 today at 5 percent, you would have $\$100 + \$5 + 5.25 = \$100\ (1 + 0.05)^2 = \$110.25$ at the end of two years. Similarly you would have $100\ (1 + 0.05)^n$ at the end of n years. In general a sum of $\$P$ will accumulate to $\$P\ (1 + r)^n$ at the end of n years where r is the interest rate expressed as a fraction.

Corporate bonds represent the first claim on the net income of a corporation and on this account are looked upon as relatively safe investments (though not quite as safe as government bonds of major countries). Some stocks are more risky. Stocks bought on, say, the New York Stock Exchange or the Paris Bourse are claims to future profits; the dollar or franc sums you receive vary with the profits of the company. From firms whose stocks yield fairly secure and stable dividends, such as American Telephone and Telegraph or General Motors, you get an almost certain but low rate of return of perhaps 5 percent. With a risky company the range of variation is higher, and you may get as much as 10 percent or as little as nil. From very risky companies you may make 50 percent on your investment for a couple of years, but you also run the risk of losing your entire capital if the company goes bankrupt.

Businesses are continually engaged in purchasing capital goods to expand their operations. They issue securities (borrow) and with the proceeds, as well as with retained profits, finance the purchase of capital goods—buildings, machines, or real assets' of other corporations—continually calculating the benefits of the investment measured against costs. It is more profitable to undertake longer-term investment when the interest rate is low than when it is high, other things remaining the same,* just as capital expansion is more profitable when business prospects are good than when the economy is in a recession.

Quite apart from the decision to buy a house or a stock or bond, the typical couple have numerous other investment chances. As they mature, they see alternative investment prospects come and go, some of which can enrich their lives and increase enjoyment and some of which can increase their future earning power. An investment in travel seems like a not very tangible kind of investment, but it is an investment all the same; it may provide both a vacation and a form of education, having a payoff in immediate enjoyment, future productivity (because today's relaxation may improve the quality of tomorrow's output), and memories of one sort or another. An investment in a hobby that costs time and money today may yield rewards in future personal satisfaction. An investment in training related to work—technical education, a computer course, a typing class—can directly add to earning power in the future.

Children represent a special type of investment. They are expected to yield future enjoyments to the couple and the feeling of gratification derived from an investment in the continuation of society. Planning a child's education and financing its cost constitute an investment in the child's future, the benefits accruing to the child himself, his parents, and indirectly to society. All these decisions fall within the category of investment strategy and illustrate an additional aspect of investment as an act of choice.

* When the interest rate goes down, businesses discount the future at a lower rate, so that the value of capital goods that yield output for a long time in the future goes up; this means that the average price of a given capital stock rises, encouraging more production of capital goods until extra production is choked off by diminishing returns in the capital-goods industries.

Investment strategy is one of the great life games of a choice unit, implicit in all choices connected with the future. A high school student investing in a college education gives up earning power for four or more years and in addition may have to borrow money for current expenses and tuition unless he can get a scholarship or aid from the state. He must weigh the cost of his investment against the value to him of the education he is likely to get—the higher income it is likely to give him, the improvement in his social status, and other emoluments of success, as well as personal satisfactions arising from a wider perspective of understanding.

Society may in fact help him to pay for his education in whole or in part, because some of the gains from his education will accrue to society as a whole—a society of educated citizens is better than one of illiterates. The social question is whether, at the margin, the transfer of a dollar from noneducational to educational spending would improve social welfare. But even if society does not subsidize our student's higher education, he may find that the monetary rate of return on investment in a college education, if he is a bright student, is in excess of the interest rate he will have to pay on borrowed money; it may, therefore, pay him to work and borrow money needed for college even if he has to finance himself without scholarship aid or government subsidy.

Investment in physical fitness is another kind of investment. Like a machine, a human being requires upkeep and daily maintenance. An investment in physical fitness may lengthen life and the productivity of current activity, providing to the individual an enlarged stream of future benefits; and part of the gains from this investment will spill over to society as a whole.

Physical and mental depreciation are partly a consequence of improper maintenance though, like machines, they eventually wear out. A man can perhaps get drunk pleasurably today and pay the price of a hangover the next day; this activity is an investment—the purchase of a current sensation for a sum of money today and psychic cost the next day. Cigarette smoking is an investment in a current pleasure that may shorten one's life. Some types of drugs may provide exhilaration today, but the costs of addiction can cause serious damage to the individual and to society in the future.

The act of choosing a mate is partly an economic act involving time and requiring investment strategy. This is obvious in some African societies, where brides may be purchased like machines and where bride wealth is an important component in a wealth holder's portfolio. But there is an important sense in which it is true in any society. There are benefits and costs in marriage. Beauty, intelligence, character, wealth, and personality are all assets traded off against one another on the margin of choice. The decision to marry involves weighing a stream of benefits against a stream of costs over time. An investment in a wife or husband is as much a part of dynamic choice as any other act of investment.

Even the choice of a President by the citizens of a nation is a gamble based on the stream of expected benefits to the individual and society during the President's tenure in office measured against the possible damage he may do to the family, the community, and the welfare of the nation.

8. *The Market and Equilibrium*

A market is a mysterious thing. You may find one on a street corner, in a city square, over the telephone, through a telegraph wire, or under the table. But a market is not a geographic location, nor is it even an institution. The market is an abstract concept. It is the domain where transactions are negotiated and prices are determined. There are many types of markets.

There are broad markets, thin markets
Stable markets, big ones.
There are fish markets, flea markets
Gem markets and then some:
Gold markets, money markets
Flesh markets, gyrating ones;
Free markets, dope markets
Controlled markets, sloppy ones.

What a lot of markets there are!

There are black markets, gray markets
Job markets, sticky ones;
Shadow markets, ghost markets
Vice markets, baby ones!

There are bond markets, bill markets
Flexible markets, monopolized ones;
Stock markets, flow markets
Put-and-call markets, curb ones.

We could go on and on:

Auction markets, betting markets,
Markets made for barter;
Demand-determined, supply-determined
Markets run by charter.
Factor markets, supermarkets
Active markets, French ones
Futures markets, spot markets
Capital markets, resilient ones.

There are even markets for presidents.

All markets have two sides, buyers and sellers. The buyers take goods off the market, the sellers put goods on the market. But every buyer is at the same time a seller, since his demand for a good is made effective by his offer of something else in exchange for it. By the same token every seller is at the same time a buyer, since his offer of something to the market implies the demand for something in exchange. The demand for fish implies the offer of something (usually money) in exchange for it; the supply of fish implies the demand for a payment of something (usually money) in return for it.

In barter markets, where there is no common thing used as money, sellers have to spend a great deal of time looking for profitable exchanges. But this system of trade, which takes great skill, is a primitive one and, as we considered in detail in Chapter 6, is an inefficient way of matching demands and supplies; efficient trade in many products requires the medium of money. In an economic system in which there is a money medium of exchange demand for a product implies an offer of money for it, while supply of a product implies a demand for money in exchange.

Market price is determined by demand and supply. Sellers offer products for money, and buyers offer money for products. When a given price is expected to prevail, a given quantity will be supplied, and a given quantity will be demanded. When the quantity supplied exceeds the quantity demanded, the price of the commodity in terms of money will be falling; to say the same thing in a slightly different way, when the money demanded by the sellers for a product exceeds the money offered by buyers for it, the value of the money in terms of the commodity will be rising. Similarly, when the quantity demanded at a given price exceeds the quantity supplied, the price of the commodity in terms of money will be rising; again, we could say that when the money offered by buyers exceeds the money demanded by sellers, the value of the money expressed in terms of the commodity will be falling.

Market equilibrium is established when demand equals supply; the price prevailing at this time is the equilibrium price. The equilibrium price is the price at which markets are cleared.

The process by which equilibrium price is reached is not necessarily a simple one, nor is it the same in all kinds of markets. Different adjustment processes are applicable to different markets.

In some markets temporary prices are set by intermediaries—brokers, specialists, or middlemen—who buy up goods from the mass of sellers and sell the goods to the mass of buyers. A village grocer acts as a middleman between farmers and consumers, buying up vegetables from farmers and selling vegetables to housewives, taking in money from housewives and paying money to farmers.

But a storekeeper also holds inventories. A given price for, say, tomatoes may rule on a given day, and at this price (adjusted by a mark-up to enable the grocer to make enough of a profit to stay in business) farmers sell what they want, and housewives buy what they want. When on a given day the quantity sold by producers exceeds the quantity bought by consumers, the inventories of the grocery rise; to reduce them, the grocer may lower the price the next day to encourage demand and to discourage supply. And when the opposite happens—when housewives buy more than the farmers are selling—the inventories of the store go down, and the grocer will put up the price. In this way market price will be continually adjusted in order to equilibrate demand and supply.

In some markets the price is adjusted quickly to maintain balance between demand and supply because intermediaries are reluctant to allow their inventories to fluctuate greatly. This is the case on the New York Stock Exchange, which is highly sensitive, even on an hour-to-hour basis, to fluctuations in demand and supply; to be sure, there are specialists in the market who hold stocks to even out fluctuations, but these specialists, in such a volatile market, do not like to build up large positions entailing great risks. It is also the case in markets for basic foodstuffs like sugar and coffee and metals like copper and zinc. It is again the case in markets for some perishable commodities, such as fish, in locations where refrigeration facilities are not available. Prices in all these markets adjust quickly to equilibrate demand and supply.

In other markets the price is adjusted very slowly and may remain constant for long periods of time. The prices of telephone services, water, electricity, gas, public transportation—public utilities in general—remain constant for long intervals, and whether privately or publicly owned are usually regulated to some extent by the government. In these markets, prices are set to cover costs and allow a normal return on the capital invested in the industry, while quantities are adjusted to make supply match the demand at the set price.

In markets for many manufactured goods prices may be set periodically while production is adjusted to the demand prevailing at the going price. Thus in the automobile markets list prices are generally established at the beginning of the automobile year, that is, at the time of the year when the new models are presented for sale to the public, while production is increased or decreased according to whether automobile stocks in the hands of car dealers are running down or piling up. This process of adjustment applies to steel and other major industries where production can be readily adjusted to demand, where there are only a few big producers in the market, and where the goods involved are durable and storable.

It is sometimes thought that price-fixing makes the law of supply and demand inapplicable. But this is not true. Prices can be fixed only insofar as supply and demand can be controlled—only insofar as the quantity of goods put on the market can be fixed in relation to the amount of money offered on the market in exchange for the goods. This is because, in a sense, the amount of goods put on the market always exchanges for the amount of money (or other goods) offered for it.

The concept of a discrepancy between demand and supply is a sensible notion infinitely appealing to common sense. But in this other sense in which "demand and supply" is used, demand and supply are equal *at every instant of time.* Distinguishing between the two senses of the phrase helps to clarify the process of market adjustment.

In the general sense in which demand and supply are always equal, the quantity put into the market (realized supply) always equals the money put into the market in exchange for it (realized demand), the ratio of the two exchanges always determining—indeed, *defining*—market price. This can be seen even if there is an intermediary who sets the price on a given day, provided that the transactions of the intermediary are taken into account in defining the demand and supply in the market.

Consider again the car market where prices are set by the auto producers at the beginning of the auto year. In this market, as in every other, realized demand is equal to actual supply. The price is set, dealers offer cars on the market, and consumers take cars off the market. The number of cars being sold has to be, of course, the same as the number of cars being bought. Any cars that are not sold at the going price add to the inventories of the dealers, and this addition to the dealers' inventories has to be taken into account in measuring market demand.

Now the dealers, having set a price on their cars, do indeed want to sell them at the going price. If they do not sell them all, they do not reduce their inventories as rapidly as they would like to, and, if orders from the manufacturers continue to come in, their inventories build up. This accumulation of inventories implies a demand on the part of the dealers for their own products, but it is a demand that is different from ordinary demand. To distinguish it from ordinary demand of consumers, we speak of *unwilling, involuntary,* or *reluctant* demand on the part of the dealers. Demand and supply are always equal, but part of the demand or supply at the existing price may be an unwilling demand. When unwilling demand or supply is excluded, demand and supply can be different, but when it is included, demand and supply are always the same.

Fixed prices do not always imply an adjustment of supply. At existing prices some consumers may have to do without; that is, they may want to buy but not be able to find any takers of the money they offer. Buyers then have to hoard money or shift purchases to something else. It is this aspect of price control under wartime conditions that usually makes it necessary for the government to introduce rationing as a means by which demand is artificially choked off to match supply at the controlled price. There is no realized excess demand in the market as a whole, but there is a meaningful sense, of course, in which we can speak of shortages in the market, shortages that often prompt the creation of black markets.

Governments, for one reason or another, often intervene to control some markets. I have just given the example of wartime price control; there are peacetime examples as well. Thus the

United States government and most European governments intervene in the market for many agricultural products. The government has typically set prices above those that would exist in the absence of intervention, so that the quantity that producers are willing to sell at the set price exceeds the quantity consumers are willing to buy. The difference is taken up by the government, which stockpiles agricultural commodities. Supply differs from demand when government purchases are not taken into account.

Take, as another example, foreign central banks. Most central banks fix the price of their currencies (exchange rates) in relation to another currency, under present practice the dollar. They are able to do so only insofar as they can control the supply of, and demand for, their currencies. To keep the dollar price of its currency fixed, a foreign central bank makes a standing offer to buy or sell its currency in exchange for dollars (which the central bank keeps in reserve). In this way the central bank acts as an intermediary. When more currency is supplied to the market than is demanded from it, the price of the currency would fall in terms of the dollar if the central bank did not step in to buy up the excess currency, itself supplying the needed number of dollars to the market. But the central bank could not indefinitely supply dollars to the market unless it had an indefinitely large supply. If it ran out of dollars, it would no longer be in a position to fix the price, and the currency would depreciate in value.

As yet another example consider the gold market. The most important gold market is in London; there are less important markets in Paris and Zurich, and there are black markets in Bombay and Karachi. The world price of gold in the (relatively) free London market is dominated by United States gold policy. Since 1934 the United States government has fixed the price of gold at $35 an ounce, buying it (for monetary purposes) when the private supply exceeds the demand and selling it when the demand exceeds the supply. In recent years the demand, including the demand of foreign banks, has been in excess of the supply, so that the United States gold stock has been declining. We shall go into the details of this when we consider the world's monetary system in Chapter 15; for now it is sufficient to notice that demand exceeds supply at the current price, not counting United States sales, which make up the difference. It is still meaningful to talk of a gold shortage because the United States Treasury cannot forever sell gold from its limited stocks without depleting its reserve and losing its power to dominate the market, as was the case in the silver market.

It is sometimes asked whether gold gives value to the dollar or the dollar gives gold its value. This question is made vague and ambiguous by the use of the term "value," which has philosophical connotations outside economics. Traditional supporters of the gold standard like to say that the value of the dollar rests on its convertibility into gold, whereas some American economists like to say that gold keeps its value because of its convertibility into the dollar, and the dollar is both a national money and the most important international currency reserve.

The only correct statement, however, is that which comes to us from the law of demand and supply. Because gold is used as international monetary reserves, the demand for it is higher than it would be if it were demonetized. The demand for gold is high among the world central banks partly because they have been traditionally willing to hold it in their reserves and partly because the United States, as the world's richest power, has always been willing to buy it in exchange for dollars.

However, the demand for dollars in international reserves has been high in relation to gold partly because the United States has, since 1934, been willing to convert dollars into gold for the monetary purposes of foreign central banks. So long as confidence in convertibility of gold into dollars is preserved, gold and dollars can be used interchangeably as international reserves. Thus there is a mutual interaction in which the acceptability of gold as a monetary reserve is enhanced by its convertibility into dollars and the acceptability of the dollar as an international money is enhanced by its convertibility into gold.

One way of making the question more precise would be to ask what would happen to the price of gold relative to dollars if the United States Treasury abandoned its policy of fixing the price of gold, neither buying it nor selling it.

The answer would depend on the policies of foreign central banks. If they kept their exchange rates fixed in relation to the dollar, they would have to buy up and hold all excess dollars on the exchange market, and speculators would have to take a position on whether foreign central banks were going to demonetize gold in the future or fix their currencies relative to it. The price of gold might rise or fall in terms of the dollar.

But if we should instead ask what would happen to the dollar price of gold if the United States and the other monetary authorities abandoned all dealings in gold for the indefinite future, it would be quite easy to predict a fall in the price of gold relative to the dollar since a substantial part of the private demand for gold is based on a guess that its price will rise.

The final question is this: What if all monetary authorities abandoned intervention not only in the gold market but also in the foreign-exchange markets? The answer is again an easy one: The price of many European currencies would rise a little relative to the dollar, and the price of gold would fall somewhat. Its role as international money having been jettisoned, gold would be relegated to the status of any other commodity.

So much for the gold market. As a last example—this time of a highly organized market—in which there is, again, official intervention—let us consider the foreign-exchange market in London. The Bank of England sets the official parity of the pound sterling at $2.80 but lets the price of a pound in terms of dollars fluctuate between $2.78 and $2.82. This means that the Bank of England stands ready to buy up any excess pounds on the foreign-exchange market when the dollar price of the pound drops toward $2.78 and stands ready to sell pounds whenever the dollar price of the pound rises toward $2.82. Between these points private dealers and banks take calls from all over the world for pounds or dollars in terms of scores of other currencies. The dollar and the pound are the two most important currencies, and the London foreign-exchange market is the most important foreign-exchange market in the world.

The Bank of England intervenes in the foreign-exchange market not only at the *support points* of $2.78 and $2.82 but also in between the support points, either because it fears a "disorderly market" or because, when sterling is weak, it is reluctant to lose dollars from its reserves and believes it can minimize losses of dollars by intervention above the pound support point of $2.78 and below the support point for the dollar of $2.82. Like the village grocery, the Bank of England acts as an intermediary in the market, facilitating the arrangements by which buyers and sellers effect legitimate transactions.

The language used by foreign-exchange dealers and operators responsible for supervising a market in which the government has a great stake may strike the outsider as unusual. One speaks of the "feel of the market," its "depth, breadth, and resiliency," "strategy of penetration," "getting in and out," "slackness," "looseness," and the market "drying up." It is the language of market intervention, but it all sounds like a scenario for a grand seduction. Indeed, one distinguished dealer from a very important central bank likens intervention to an exercise in applied psychology and manipulation of a market to the management of a woman. When it is troubled, it must be caressed; when it is quiet, it should be left alone; and when it gets hysterical, it has to be slapped. In that sense the market is feminine.

9. *Adjustment and Competition*

Everything influences everything else. Demand and supply of a good depend on its price, but also on the prices of related products. The demand and supply of lettuce depend on the price of lettuce but also on the prices of tomatoes, salt, and other things. The price of lettuce affects the price of tomatoes, which in turn influences the price of salt, the wages of middlemen, and household cash balances. The price of theater tickets affects the income of actors, which influences the supply of movies, which affects the sale of pop records and eventually the British balance of payments. Money flows through one market into another constantly affecting demands, supplies, and prices, the budgets of members of the community, the taxes owed and paid, and even, very indirectly, the form of government elected.

These direct and indirect relationships can best be seen by examining and elaborating on the forces influencing market price.

Normally, the quantity of a product demanded decreases when the price rises and increases when the price falls, while the quantity supplied increases when the price rises and decreases when the price falls. This means that a price above equilibrium usually makes demand less than supply, while a decrease in price usually makes supply less than demand.

Starting from an equilibrium price, any changes that alter demand or supply conditions will generate a new equilibrium price. An increase in demand for a good will cause a higher price, and a decrease in demand will cause a lower price. Similarly, an increase in supply will cause a lower price, and a decrease in supply will cause a higher price. Demand and supply of a good are affected, as I have said, not only by the price of the good but by the prices of competing goods. Suppose a housewife goes to the market on a particular day with the idea of buying a certain quantity of tomatoes and a certain quantity of lettuce on the expectation that prices will be the same as yesterday. But suppose she finds that the price of lettuce has gone up. This change in price will probably induce her to buy a larger quantity of tomatoes and a smaller quantity of lettuce than she had planned; she will probably *substitute* tomatoes for lettuce. Lettuce and tomatoes are substitutes for one another in consumption, and this means that the higher the price of one, the more you buy of the other.

Goods satisfying similar wants are *substitutes.* Thus carrots and spinach are substitutes for one another; so are pork, ham, lamb, and beef, movies, television, and radio, train rides, airplane rides, and bus rides, and bourbon and Scotch. An increase in the price of one shifts demand onto others. Substitute goods compete with one another in the elimination of wants.

Complements are another class of goods. A good is complementary to another good if the two goods are used together, in tandem, so to speak. If an increase in the price of a complement reduces demand for it, it also reduces demand for a good complementary to it. Thus left and right shoes are complements; so are bread and butter, gasoline and tires, cold weather and overcoats, bathing suits and beaches, and coffee and cream (or coffee and cognac).

An increase in the amount of a good supplied usually lowers its price and shifts demand onto the good. But there are indirect effects that increase demand for complementary goods and decrease demand for substitute goods. Thus an increase in the supply of lettuce will lower its price and increase the quantity bought. But it will also increase the demand for salt (lettuce and salt are complements) and perhaps increase its price a little also. There are still more indirect effects, for the decrease in the price of lettuce may decrease the demand for tomatoes (because lettuce and tomatoes are substitutes) and cause a reduction in the price of tomatoes, which in turn will reduce the overall extent to which demand is shifted away from tomatoes. In turn the smaller equilibrium quantity of tomatoes bought may result in a smaller demand for salt (salt is also complementary to tomatoes). You could not, therefore, be certain about the final effect of the original change in the supply conditions of the lettuce market on the price of salt.

Supply and demand are completely general concepts, and so is price. Of course you may not find it helpful to think in economic terms, express yourself in the quaint language of economics, or apply economic concepts to ordinary life. It is nevertheless useful to see that these concepts do apply generally.

Suppose that there are five men and five women in a night club and that each has come without a partner. The chances are that at least some partnerships will be formed. Now suppose the number of men increases to ten. Will you not see a progressive alternative in the "price," or "exchange value," of men in relation to women? Will not the "price" of men go down relative to the "price" of women? The range of choice is widened for the women, and the competition among the men becomes more assiduous; the attention received by each woman will increase—one of the implicit dimensions of the concept of price.

But now suppose word gets around in our club with five women and ten men that in a nearby bar there are ten women and only five men. One club has a comparative advantage in men, the other in women, and opportunities for profitable trades or migration arise. Initially we have two isolated markets, but then the markets become connected. Men flow from the bar where they are in abundance and the "price" low, and women flow in the opposite direction, until a new equilibrium is established. The equilibrium solution is to have in each bar an equal number of men and women.

In this market men (and women) are substitutes for one another, but men are complementary to women. Suppose, therefore, that one woman in the first club retires for the evening—alone. According to the principle established above, this should raise the "price" of the other women in both clubs, since they are substitutes, and decrease the "price" of men because they are complements—a process which would indeed fit in most cases the facts of experience.

We find analogous applications of the principle of supply and demand in all walks of life. The political process can be looked upon as a market. Political candidates try to market their services in competition for a seat in the government. When the supply of attractive candidates increases, there develops a buyer's market, looked at from the point of view of the constituency, and the competition becomes more intense. An election and an auction market have many fundamental similarities underlying their superficial differences in form.

The principles of supply and demand even apply to conversation. It is sometimes said that talk is cheap because the supply exceeds the demand. If the supply of talk exceeds the demand for it, its price falls, as it were, and people move away. On the other hand, awkward silences are expressions of an excess demand for talk; the utility of a few words increases sharply, so that silences are gratefully filled even if no party has anything sensible to say.

Hosts and hostesses at cocktail parties, typically a forum for conversation, act partly in the role of conversation brokers, just as real estate brokers bring suppliers and demanders together in the housing market and the referee brings opposing sides of a hockey game together.

Beneath the formality of the price-determining forces of demand and supply lies *competition,* the great regulator, along with *custom,* of market activity. The degree of competition, ranging from the atomistic wheat market to the great monopolies, has a vital bearing on the development of economic and social institutions.

Every decision unit has control over the things it possesses and the exchanges it *offers* to make. In a sense, every seller is a monopolist of the goods he himself has to sell, and every buyer is a monopolist of the goods he himself wants to buy. This does not, however, imply very much about the range of the goods available to the potential buyer or the range of buyers competing for the services of the seller.

Consider, for example, a construction worker whose work is not very different from the work of many others. He is a monopolist in the sense that he can withhold his own labor from the market, but he cannot charge a price for his services that is much higher than the price prevailing in the market for other workers of like ability. If he attempts to do so, he will not be able to sell his services; he will have priced himself out of the market.

But suppose that our construction worker is a man of exceptional ability. Suppose he can perform services over and above what his competitors perform; the services of other workers are very imperfect substitutes for his own work. Then employers of construction workers will compete for *his* services and be willing to pay a premium for them over and above what is paid the ordinary run of construction workers. The premium that is paid him is based on his monopoly of additional talent or productivity for which he can command a *monopoly rent.*

The term *rent* originates in Ricardo's analysis of land. High-quality land commands the highest rent, the next highest grade the next highest rent, and so on; marginal land would command no rent at all and would be sold for a zero price.

The concept of rent is strictly applicable to workmen of different quality. The best workmen in a free market will receive the highest wages, the second best the second highest, and so on, until the marginal workers will command the ordinary wage received by men of common ability. (In principle the marginal worker could receive a zero wage, like marginal land, but a worker, unlike land, requires upkeep and a wage below subsistence would result in his retirement from the work force, and indeed, human existence.)

Institutions however (such as labor unions) or legal restrictions (for example, standardized wage laws) can interfere with this natural process by stimulating what amounts to a collective monopoly cartel and enforcing standardized pay scales for men regardless of their different abilities and productivity.

Among workmen anyone with services to offer is included. Frank Sinatra commands a monopoly rent because of the quality of his voice, his acting ability, or other attributes of his personality. Exceptional scientists, artists, and writers may command monopoly rents because of the uniqueness and marketability of their talents. Monopoly is an attribute of the uniqueness of any service.

An analogous situation applies to *monopsonists*. A monopsonist is a single buyer. Governments are monopsonists in the market for military hardware. A monopsonist commands a *monopsony rent* in the sense that he may be able to buy a good for a far lower price than he would, even in the absence of his uniqueness, be willing to pay; by threatening to buy a smaller quantity or withdraw his patronage, he may be able to force the sellers to lower their prices; that is to say, by artificially reducing, or threatening to reduce, demand, he can make the price fall.

The extent of monopoly or monopsony power depends on the competition of alternative substitutes. A singer may have the best voice, but if there are other singers nearly as good, his power to exploit his monopoly is limited; if there are many others just as good, he will not be able to charge a higher price than that ruling in the market. Similarly, the earnings of movie stars will be influenced by the earnings of competing actors, and the earnings of artists will be affected by the earnings of other artists producing close substitutes. In art and science, of course, originality and innovation play a large part, and substitution may be quite difficult.

The forces of competition affecting the earnings of individuals also apply to the earnings of firms. A company may command a large share of the market for a particular type of cheese or car, but the rent that can be charged on account of the uniqueness of the product will be affected by the supply of close substitutes. A company controlling the market for aluminum will still have to compete with producers of steel and alloys that can be substituted for aluminum. Even painters have to compete in an indirect way with musicians in the sense that while music and painting are distinct and separate aesthetic forms, substitution of enjoyment of one for enjoyment of the other is to some extent possible.

Competition can take two forms, a personal and an impersonal form. Competition is personal when the competitors can be readily identified and singled out; it is impersonal when they cannot.

A good example of an impersonal market is the market for wheat. There are different grades of wheat, but the market for each grade is a unified market. There are thousands of wheat producers, and there is a single price for wheat delivered at a given time at a given place. The wheat market is impersonal because while every wheat producer competes with every other producer, each one acting alone has little or no influence on the market price because of the insignificant size of his share; his competitors likewise, acting singly, have no influence on price. Thus even though one wheat farmer is in competition with wheat farmers in general, he does not regard himself as harmed by the success of his neighbors.

Competition is personal, on the other hand, when competitors are readily identified as unique entities. Under personal competition one producer is distinctly affected by the success of other recognizable producers. The Hertz and Avis car-rental companies are classic cases of personal competition.

What determines whether there are many competitors in an industry or few competitors? A major determinant is the technology determining the efficient size of the plants and firms in an industry in relation to the size of the market. In some industries, such as the automobile industry, firms producing on a small scale of production can only do so at high cost. As output expands, average costs of production fall, so that even if many firms initially enter the industry, only a few will be able to survive and reap the cost advantages of large-scale production. After a point, however, the costs from further expansion rise, and decreasing returns to the management of large-scale enterprizes sets in.

The number of firms in equilibrium in an industry depends on the relation between the efficient-sized firm and the size of the market as a whole. The wheat market has many producers because the efficient-sized wheat farm is small in relation to the market; the automobile market has few competitors because the efficient firm is large in relation to the market; and most public utilities in major cities—firms providing electricity and gas, water and public transportation—are single firms because costs continually fall as output increases (technological economies of scale outweigh managerial diseconomies).

Equilibrium prices can be affected by the degree of competition. In the extreme case of public utilities (which are usually considered natural monopolies), the prices charged are generally regulated by the government, or the government itself runs the industry. In impersonal competition with many producers market price is determined and will lead, in the long run, to a price that will just enable producers to stay in business. But in the intermediate case of personal competition an element of indeterminacy exists.

The indeterminacy stems from the strategies by which prices are determined. In the case of two, three, or a few producers, the output and price policies of one are intimately affected by the output and price policies of the rival producers. Producers know that price reduction will be met by competitors, whereas price increases not matched by competitors will quickly result in a reduction in the market share of a particular firm. Experience with cutthroat competition and ruinous attempts to drive out rivals results in a *standoff,* a balance of competition in which tacit agreements are made to compete on nonprice variables. Competition, instead of taking the form of price competition, takes the more innocuous form of advertising, or quality, competition, a process in which producers try to demonstrate by advertising that the qualities of their products differ from the qualities of their rivals' products. Actual product differentiation is enhanced by independent research in the laboratories of the major companies.

Thus it is that the institutions and firms in the economy—of the city, the state, the nation, or the whole world—arrive at equilibrium sizes. Goods are supplied by industries containing firms of varying sizes, reaching a balance after the interplay of competition and rivalry drives out the inefficient and brings about an approximation to efficiency.

All aspects of human life satisfying specific desires—the production of all goods—are subject to the laws of competition. Exceptional virtues or attributes of a productive agent are paid monopoly rents, a tribute to their uniqueness. A beautiful girl, a wealthy man, or an amusing personality commands a monopoly rent in social interplay; a swimmer commands a monopoly premium in a group of survivors on a life raft; a doctor commands a monopoly premium in a society stricken by plague. Rivalry among people is affected by numbers. In a university class of hundreds where examinations are graded on a curve, competition is impersonal, and small groups can work together for their mutual improvement. But in smaller classes where the same principle applies, friendship is tested in a tougher way, since a friend's "A" may be your "C." Personal competition thus has its vicious features.

II. *Problems*

10. *Inflation and Money*

Just as the price of a single commodity is determined by the demand and supply in the corresponding market, so the general price level—the average price of commodities, or the value of money—is determined by *aggregate demand* and *aggregate supply,* that is, the sum of the demands for individual products and the sum of the supplies of them. When aggregate demand increases or aggregate supply decreases, the price level rises; when aggregate demand decreases or aggregate supply increases, the price level falls.

The levels of aggregate demand and aggregate supply are closely related to the monetary system. We have already seen how individuals have a need for liquidity, a need to keep a sum of money in their pockets or in the bank for ordinary transactions and in addition a certain extra balance in a savings account to meet contingencies and to take advantage of sudden speculative opportunities. We have also seen how, when individuals become excessively liquid, they spend their excess cash either on durable goods or on stocks, bonds, or other financial assets. Now when all the inhabitants of the community, taken as a whole, have more liquidity than they want, buyers go to the market with more money to spend on goods and securities than sellers have commodities and securities to sell. The excess of offers to buy over offers to sell means that the price of goods and securities rises. There is "too much money chasing too few goods," so the value of the existing stock of money has to fall.

Similarly, when the community as a whole is short of liquidity, there is a general attempt to conserve cash. Sellers go to the market with more goods and securities than buyers want to spend money on. The community as a whole tries to build up a cash balance, but since the community cannot, collectively, sell more than it buys, the attempt to sell more results in a fall in the price level. There is "too little money chasing too many goods," so the value of the existing stock of money has to rise.

For any given level of liquidity in the community there is only one possible equilibrium level of prices. The higher is the stock of liquidity, the higher is the equilibrium price level.

To see why this is so, suppose that the price of all things, including wages and all assets, is doubled overnight, as if by a miracle. Can the price level remain at this inflated level?

The answer is no. Each spending unit—every individual, household, and firm—will find that the nominal amount of money in the pocket and in the bank remains as before, but the prices of all things have doubled. In terms of dollars the money a man has is the same as before, but in terms of the things dollars will buy, his liquidity has fallen in half. Supposing that every spender was in equilibrium before the price change occurred, not one is in equilibrium now; each will therefore try to build back his liquidity to the point where he has the same command over goods as before. He will check his spending, offering more on the market than he wants to buy; and similar action by all members of the community will ensure a general oversupply of commodities and securities, a scarcity of money, and a fall in the price level. The price level will march right back down to where it was before. Our "miraculous" experiment is not a very durable miracle.

The opposite happens if the price level, again as if by a miracle, falls while the money in people's hands and in the bank remains unchanged. With the prices of commodities half of what they were before, people with the same number of dollars in their pockets or the bank find that the dollars buy twice what they formerly bought. Liquidity in terms of command over commodities is double its previous amount, and each buyer will spend it in the attempt to use resources more profitably. There will be a general excess of buying over selling, and the price level will go back up to where it was before.

In these cases we have supposed that the amount of money in the hands of the community remains unchanged, and we have seen how this ensures a single price level appropriate to that quantity of money. In both cases, when we moved the price level away from equilibrium, the original level was restored.

If the amount of money is itself changed, the equilibrium level of prices will be altered more or less in proportion to the change in the quantity of money. Let us suppose this time that "miraculously" (though, as we shall see, governments can perform this "miracle"), the quantity of dollars in the hands or bank account of each spender doubles. Suppose the community was initially in equilibrium; it cannot be any longer, because liquidity will now be doubled. In the effort to reduce excess cash (because it is profitable to make investments with it), the community tries to buy more than it sells. But as we have seen, the attempt to buy more goods than are available simply bids up prices. Since the community as a whole cannot (or will not) destroy the number of dollars in existence, the real value of the dollars will go down. The price level will double and the value of liquidity be the same as it was before the "miraculous" doubling of the supply of cash.

Exactly the opposite happens if prices are flexible and the stock of money is reduced; households and firms get short of cash and attempt to rebuild liquidity by reducing spending. Given a reduced supply of dollars, the only way the community as a whole can restore its liquidity is by lowering the price level;

the price level will fall (if it is flexible enough) more or less in proportion to the stock of money.*

We can now see how a given price level corresponds to a given stock of money. Increasing the money supply will raise the price level, lowering it will lower the price level—a conclusion we should expect from a straightforward application of the law of demand and supply applied to any market. Great inflations (persistent increases in the general price level) and great deflations (persistent declines in the price level) are always associated with great increases or decreases in the quantity of money.†

There are many examples of widespread movements in the price level in ancient and modern times. Before modern times the main device by which money (which was largely in the form of gold and silver) was increased was through a change in the face value of the coins minted by governments. It was usual in ancient Greece and Rome, in Europe and in Asia in the Middle Ages for the government to set its seal on pieces of gold and silver to verify the weight and fineness of the resulting coin. The precious metal was the raw material out of which money in the form of coins was struck. Now the sovereign—emperor, king, sultan, or prince—could often not resist the temptation to water down the coinage—to devalue it—by printing a higher face value on the coinage than its metallic content warranted. For a given sum of gold and silver he would issue, say, 110 coins instead of 100 coins, using the remainder to finance his personal expenses or the expenses of his kingdom. The increase in the supply of, say, English shillings would raise

* In the next chapter we shall go into the problems of depression that result when prices and wages are not flexible.

† The relationship between money and prices is not exact at any moment of time, of course, because money can turn over faster from one period to the next. But after all adjustments have taken place and the rate at which money turns over has been restored to its equilibrium level, the relationship is valid.

the prices of commodities relative to shillings more or less in proportion to the increase in shilling coins, even though the total metallic content was unchanged; the value of a shilling would then fall. The metallic value of commodities stayed the same, but shilling prices rose, since the metallic content of the shilling was diminished.

As banking progressed and paper money became increasingly substituted for metallic money in ordinary circulation along the lines described in Chapter 6, banks could issue notes that were convertible into gold and silver without keeping 100 percent reserves of precious metals behind their paper issues. Without these money substitutes the price level would have fallen over time in order to raise the commodity value of gold and silver. This is because more liquidity is needed as economies expand; money has more work to do. But as long as convertibility of paper into money was maintained, there was a limit to the extent to which private banks, and later central banks, could issue paper. If they went too far, the public would lose confidence in them, withdraw deposits, and bring about their collapse; the paper money the banks had issued would be worthless. The consequent fall in liquidity could induce a tremendous deflation. But the important point is that the requirement of convertibility protected the public against excess issues of the banking system and the government.

With the breakdown of the gold standard after 1914, however, the requirement of convertibility of paper money into gold was in most countries abandoned. Paper money was issued by most national governments without the gold-convertibility privilege. This meant that the control of the stock of money in the economy came to rest, not on the general economic principle of convertibility, but on the basis of the authority of the government in power. Fiat money—money that is legal tender only because the government says it is—came to be more important than metallic money of intrinsic worth.

Governments have budgets like every other spender in the economy. They pay expenses and collect taxes. But the public in every country is always the same; it wants the services the government provides but does not like to pay the taxes to finance these services. The temptation of government is therefore very great indeed, in its search for popularity, to continue to increase services without financing them through corresponding increases in taxes. A government runs budget deficits and accumulates a great public debt, and the central bank, an arm of the government, buys up part of the government debt by printing more money or crediting the government with deposits at the central bank.

This process is especially common during great crises or war. In the 1914 to 1918 war one government after another required the central bank to finance a part of wartime expenses by buying up government bonds. The government would pay its extraordinary wartime expenses by issuing these bonds. These issues alone would put an enormous burden on the credit markets, since the bonds could only be sold at a lower price (below par), which meant that a higher interest rate had to be paid on money borrowed. The government bonds would compete with corporate bonds and stocks and thus drive down their prices too. (Remember our discussion about substitutes—government bonds and corporate bonds and stocks are substitutes.) In the absence of central bank financing the scarcity of liquidity of the government would be shifted partly onto the private community, and this would force businesses and households to cut back on their spending to make room for the government's spending.

This process itself would be only slightly inflationary. But a government will not ordinarily let interest rates rise to the extent implied. Instead the government pressures the central bank to buy up some of the bonds the government has issued; the central bank pays for the bonds with newly printed money or credits the government with deposits at the central bank.

When the government spends the cash it has borrowed, the cash goes first into the hands of the people and firms who have sold the government goods, and they put the money into their bank accounts or spend it directly. The addition to reserves permits the banks holding excess cash to participate in purchasing new government bond issues. But the upshot is a great increase in the liquidity of the system as a whole and an upward movement in prices.

This happened in every country in Europe during the First World War and also, to a lesser extent, in the United States. The same thing happened during the Second World War.

To be sure, the governments of most countries did put controls on prices to make supply equal to demand by rationing goods available for purchase. This held prices down while the war was on, but after it ended and the controls were lifted, the inevitable happened. Households and firms became excessively liquid during the control period, and the removal of controls after the war was like lifting the lid of the boiler. Demand exceeded supply, and prices zoomed. The controls had merely bottled up the inflationary pressure in what is usually called repressed inflation.

But inflation is not confined to wartime. In the aftermath of the First World War the defeated Central Powers had huge reconstruction expenses, and the Treaty of Versailles had saddled them with heavy reparation debts. With a greatly reduced tax base the governments could not finance all their expenditures through taxes and resorted to the printing press. In the course of a year and a half the price level in Germany and many other countries doubled, then tripled, then quadrupled, until by 1923 prices were trillions of times what they had been before the process started. The currency issued by the German Reichsbank became virtually worthless in its exchange value for commodities and on foreign-exchange markets. Today we see numerous (although less dramatic) examples of the same phenomenon at work—in Indonesia, Brazil, and other poor countries of Africa and Latin America.

The source of persistent inflation is almost always the same. Pressures for government spending are so great that it is carried beyond the capacity of the government to finance out of taxes; government debts are sold to the banks of issue which provide the government with the cash to pay the deficits, and the resulting increase in the liquidity of the community creates an excess of demand over supply and the inevitable rise in prices.

In its early stages, inflation often induces a euphoria on the part of the public. Money incomes swell, and this creates the illusion of an improvement in well-being. The husband-earner gets higher wages and puts more cash in the family till, and the wife-spender does not at once realize that the larger amount of money available for spending will not buy a larger collection of commodities. Yet the loss of income that results from the inflationary process for the community in the aggregate is indisputable. Inflation is an unmitigated nuisance.

Let us suppose, for example, that the husband-earner's salary goes up by 10 percent and that the prices of everything the wife-spender buys also rise by 10 percent. Even in this case the household is worse off, because cash holdings lose 10 percent of their commodity value, a reduction in real income that amounts to a "tax" on that part of wealth held in the form of cash. If the rise in prices is expected to be permanent but no further inflation is expected, the household will cut spending to replenish the liquidity value of its cash holdings—a reduction in spending that will release resources to other parts of the community or from the community as a whole to the government. It is this reduction in the community's spending, in its effort to replenish cash balances, that permits the government to acquire resources from the community and justifies the identification of the inflation with a tax.

If, however, the inflation is expected to continue, spenders will realize that there has been an increased cost of holding liquidity —real cash balances. If wage earnings and prices go up by, say, 10 percent *every year,* a given quantity of money balances will buy 10 percent less each year. To keep the same liquidity, the people in the community would have to acquire 10 percent more cash each year. But the cost of being liquid will have risen, and households and firms will economize on liquidity by holding a smaller quantity of command over commodities. After they have reduced their liquidity, they will still have to add 10 percent more money to their smaller *real* cash holdings each year to preserve that smaller quantity of liquidity from deteriorating further.

The fact that its members have to economize on liquidity implies a cost to the community as a whole, the cost or "waste" associated with inflation even when it is anticipated. The cost of holding a medium of exchange rises during inflation, and individuals suffer from the inconvenience of a money which now is less suitable as a medium of exchange. Perhaps they have to make more frequent trips to the bank, forgo extra safety when confronted with unexpected emergencies, or give up their *masse de manoeuvre* in case an unexpected bargain comes up. Since liquidity is also an instrument of production, it interferes with the efficiency with which shops are run and the productivity of those in the economy who try to keep the money in their till down to an irreducible minimum. Inflation on this account is a great inconvenience and, even when it is regarded as a tax, has to be considered a very inefficient form of tax. Inflation increases the cost of making transactions.

But we have only scratched the surface of the ills inflation can cause. As we have seen, a rising level of prices caused by excessive rates of monetary expansion reduces the usefulness of money as a medium of exchange even when everyone knows how rapidly money is depreciating and adapts to that fact. But the uncertainty of the general price level associated with inflation is an even greater source of harm.

We saw in Chapter 6 why money is needed as a standard for contractual obligations. But if the price level goes up one year by 10 percent, the next year by 5 percent, and the succeeding year by 20 percent, accelerating and decelerating in an arbitrary fashion, the advantages of money as a unit of contract are destroyed. It then serves its function as a unit of contract no better than would, say, sugar or coffee or copper—commodities susceptible of great variations in price even when the purchasing power of money is stable in the aggregate.

Money also serves its function less well as a unit of account during inflation, a defect of inflation quite distinct from those previously mentioned. During inflationary periods prices never go up at the same rate; some prices are relatively sluggish, while others rise quite rapidly. This means that even if buyers expect a general price rise, plans each day will be upset by the discovery that prices are jumping around, making calculations more onerous and decisions more tedious. Information costs mount.

But we have not yet come to what is surely one of the greatest evils of all—the fact that purchasing power is transferred capriciously from some parts of the community to others irrespective of the needs or valid expectations of those involved.

Let us suppose, for example, that during a period of stable prices a man and his wife purchase a house, undertaking a $25,000 mortgage on which they pay a rate of interest of 6 percent. If now all prices (including the price of houses) and wages start to go up at a rate of 6 percent and continue at that rate for the duration of their mortgage, they will find that *in terms of commodities* they have not paid any interest at all on their mortgage. While they pay a nominal interest of 6 percent a year every year, the value of the money they pay in interest depreciates by 6 percent. And if the rate of inflation exceeds

6 percent, they will in effect be paying a negative interest rate!

This may be seen more clearly if we imagine a once-for-all doubling of all prices and money incomes. The purchasing power of our couple's money income stays the same, but the price of their house will double to $50,000. However, the mortgage debt the couple have to pay back stays at $25,000, so that, at current prices, they will have gained $25,000, which is worth $12,500 in terms of commodities. The real debt they owe has been cut in half, and this is an entirely capricious gain they had not expected.

Of course it is nice to make such a profit. But this gain is somebody else's loss, and if the shoe were on the other foot, our couple wouldn't feel so happy. Consider another couple who had saved up $25,000 and conservatively put it into a savings account at the savings and loan association that lent our lucky couple the money. The purchasing power of the thrifty couple's savings would have been cut in half. The process is just the same as if they had given our lucky couple half their savings and the price level had stayed constant.

This only suggests the injustices that can be caused by inflation. Some workers earn salaries that are fixed in money terms, and the purchasing power of these salaries falls as prices rise. Workers who have put aside part of their income for a pension fixed in dollars at retirement find their pension will not allow them to lead the kind of life they had expected and felt they had a right to expect. Widows who have to live on a survivor's estate fixed in dollar terms find the purchasing power of their incomes eroded away by inflation.

Whether the result is a gain or a loss to a particular individual, the result of inflation is an entirely arbitrary redistribution of income from creditors to debtors and from the thrifty to the spendthrifts. But the gainers gain less than the losers give up so inflation results in economic waste.

11. *Unemployment and Depression*

In considering the waste and inequities associated with changes in the price level, I concentrated on the problem of inflation, although I might equally have called attention to deflation. Had I put everything in reverse, I could have shown how the house buyer loses, how the bondholder gains, and how the purchasing power of pensions or life insurance policies goes up when the price level goes down. I did not emphasize this mirror image of the inflation process because circumstances, especially in this century, have made the deflationary process take a complex course.

There is, first of all, an asymmetry between inflation and deflation. By issuing great quantities of money, the government or central bank can readily reduce its value through inflation, and the temptation for a government—especially a government that does not need to be responsive to the interests of the people—to do so is always present insofar as it can acquire goods and services from the public with the money it creates. But it is quite another thing to cause, over an extended period of time, a great deflation. In principle that could happen if the government were to run a budget surplus and reduce the quantity of money, or if the economy were to experience a sudden expansion in productivity. Bonds, denominated in dollars, would yield an increased return in commodities and become so attractive that their prices would rise, as the community tried to shift out of commodities and stocks. But there are lower limits below which the rate of interest cannot go, and these limits establish, over the long run, the maximum rate of deflation that is feasible. Except for short periods, rates of deflation in excess of the long-run rate of growth of output of an economy have never been observed.

It is true that there have been periods of mild secular deflation in history. In the middle of the nineteenth century there was an inflationary period after the great gold discoveries in America and Australia, but by 1870 the rate of gold production had declined, while world production had increased, and for twenty years there was deflation in the major countries of the world. From 1865 to 1890 deflation had a profound impact on American life and exerted great hardship on particular groups, particularly the farming classes. Up to 1873 the United States used both gold and silver as money, but in that year the government demonetized silver, contributing to further deflation.* The deflation meant that farmers who had bought land on the basis of mortgages at high interest rates found the burden of the interest payment and amortization of their debts sharply increased. (It was discontent due to the accompanying reduction in the standard of living of farmers that contributed to the Populist movement in American politics and William Jennings Bryan's famous "cross of gold" speech.) Deflation works a great hardship on the debtor class, just as inflation bears heavily on the creditor class.

Circumstances gradually changed in this century, however, and shifted the problem from deflation to something even worse—depression and unemployment.

We have seen how when the money supply is increased, excess demand is created which will cause prices and wages to rise if they are flexible and if there is not a corresponding increase in supply. But the degree of price and wage flexibility is not as great in the downward direction.

* This step also disrupted currencies of other countries of the world that were on a silver standard.

When the money supply contracts, the community becomes starved for liquidity, reduces its offers to buy and lend, and increases its offers to sell and borrow. Excess supply of commodities, securities, and labor is created, and prices of commodities and the wages of labor would fall if they are flexible, while interest rates go up (security prices go down).

If all wages and prices were flexible in both directions, this deflationary process resulting from excess supply would mirror the inflationary price movement when there is excess demand. But in the modern age prices and wage rates are sluggish in responding downward to excess supply. Excess supply tends to cause a reduction of output and unemployment more than it tends to cause a fall in prices and wages.

When the demand for automobiles falls off and the inventories of car dealers pile up, competition for sales becomes more fierce, and bargains are offered. But there is a limit to the extent to which prices can fall without dealers going out of business. Dealers cut back on orders from the producers, who, instead of cutting prices, reduce the work week or lay off workers and close down particular plants. The first impact of general excess supply of commodities (and excess demand for liquidity) in the industrial sector of the economy falls on output and employment rather than on prices and wages.

The reduction in output can quickly spread. Auto producers lay off workers and reduce orders from steel plants, subcontractors, and utility companies; steel producers in turn lay off steel workers, reduce orders from iron industries and other suppliers, and cut back their own production. Meanwhile auto workers and steel workers who have become unemployed or underemployed have to cut back spending on luxuries and even some necessities, spreading the recession process from department stores to the local shopkeeper and back to the worker.

The construction industries may be particularly heavily hit. In the initial stages of excess supply (when there is excess supply of securities in the scramble for liquidity) interest rates rise, increasing the difficulty and cost of financing purchases of durable goods and reducing orders for new houses. Construction activity is thus postponed, reducing demand for the products of the construction industries besides creating unemployment among construction workers.

In these ways recession spreads, becoming depression, a state of the economy that causes generalized hardships out of all proportion to the initial decrease in demand—hardships in which business, labor, and farmers share. Few people gain from depression.

A fall in wage rates would work in the direction of correcting the excess supply and restoring equilibrium, partly because it would stimulate substitution of labor services for the services of other factors, and partly because it raises the labor services value of cash balances. But wage contracts in modern industrial society are set for long periods—sometimes for a year, sometimes for three years—and the hard-fought increases of salary in union-management negotiations are not lightly given up. By the time the consequences of the excess supply have spread throughout the economy, before wage reductions would do much good to restore a new balance in the economy at full employment, business confidence in the further growth of demand has been shattered, and spending on investment projects is cut back, further reinforcing the depression of the economy.

This devastating downward process actually occurred in the United States (and the world) economy after the stock-market crash of 1929. At that time overinvestment and speculative fever had bid up stock prices to unprecedented and unrealistic proportions. Stock-market speculators were buying claims to future profit streams that could not possibly materialize. As a result of the new output made possible by the preceding investment boom, inventories began to rise in the middle of 1929, and the public began to have second thoughts on the profits to be made in the stock market. When the stock market stopped rising in September, those who had bought on the expectation of further increase stopped buying and began to liquidate their holdings. Within a month pessimism and uncertainty had become widespread, and there was a flight from stocks to bonds and cash, culminating in the agony of Black Friday, when "the bottom dropped out of the market." Panic selling intensified the process and the downward trend of the market continued despite attempts—rather halfhearted, to be sure—by business leaders, banks, and the government to stabilize it. Within a few months the public was aware of the Great Depression in the making, and unemployment began to rise to alarming proportions. Uncertainty spread throughout the economy, and the banks became infected. The soundness of the banks began to be questioned, and withdrawals caused one bank failure after another, destroying the monetary basis on which liquidity was founded. By 1931 the Depression in the United States had spread all around the world, forcing Britain off the gold standard, and stirring a wave of currency devaluations. By 1933 the banking system in this country had become completely demoralized and bank doors were closed to depositors in the moratorium that was President Roosevelt's first act after his inauguration.

The Great Depression lasted for ten years, although the worst was over in 1934. In the United States the breakdown of production and mass unemployment that lasted until the outbreak of the Second World War exacted toll in terms of poverty, misery, and disruption that is almost unimaginable to those who did not live through the Depression. Its impact on the rest of the world created the conditions that allowed fascism to thrive and thus set the stage for Hitler's war.

The Great Depression affected the government institutions of the major countries and brought to the forefront the responsibility of the government for preserving the stability of the economy. Today every government regards itself as responsible for the prevention of severe depressions and the control of inflation. Government has to formulate economic policy to prevent or ameliorate the ups and downs of economic activity and prices. Depressions, as we have seen, start off as an excess of supply over demand, while inflation is an excess of demand over supply. The problem of government policy, therefore, is to manage aggregate demand and supply so as to eliminate excess supply during a depression and excess demand during inflation.

The government has, broadly, two means of increasing or decreasing demand: fiscal policy and monetary policy. Fiscal policy involves the relation between government spending and taxes. When the government increases expenditures, it adds directly to the demand for the goods it buys; and when it lowers taxes, it reduces the amount of money the taxpayers have to pay to the government and thus encourages additional spending on the part of the taxpayers. Similarly, when the government lowers its own direct spending or raises taxes, it reduces the aggregate demand for goods in the economy.

Monetary policy is the other great weapon of stabilization policy, although it cannot be used in disregard of the need for preserving the international value of a currency. When the central bank (in the United States the Federal Reserve System) buys assets (usually government bonds), it creates money because it pays for assets by new issues of currency or reserves for the banking system. The recipients of the money, the people who have sold the government bonds to the central bank, then become more liquid and put part of the added cash in banks, increasing bank reserves and permitting the commercial banks to reduce interest rates and lend more. The economy as a whole becomes more liquid, and spending is increased.

Contraction of the money supply through central bank sales of assets (or raising the reserve requirements of the commercial banks) has just the opposite effect. It decreases liquidity, forcing the public to economize on private spending, and therefore reduces excess demand.

It is important to recognize, however, an asymmetry in the process by which monetary policy works. When a man's liquidity is sharply reduced, he will be *forced* to cut down his spending if he is to remain solvent, whereas when a man's liquidity is increased, he is only *enabled* to increase his spending. You can always keep a horse away from the water trough. But when you lead a horse to water, you can't make him drink. Somewhat similarly the central bank can stop a boom easier than it can correct a depression. It takes more time to correct a recession or depression, insofar as monetary policy is concerned, especially if business confidence has been seriously upset.

It is partly for this reason that governments usually have to combine monetary and fiscal policy in the management of aggregate demand. In a deep depression a government would be quite correct in allowing tax reductions to encourage additional private spending and also correct in encouraging (or requiring) the central bank to buy assets and increase the money supply in order to ensure that the economy as a whole, including the government, had an ample supply of liquidity. For related reasons inflation can be prevented by a proper restraint on the money supply combined with a more frugal approach to public spending that is not financed out of taxes.

Once an economy is on an even path of growth, with the money supply expanding at a suitable rate (roughly corresponding to the growth of output) and productive factors more or less fully employed, it is necessary that the government manage its affairs in such a way that stability is maintained. Moderate government budget surpluses and deficits are inevitable for any government of an economy subject to business cycles, but careful attention to sound monetary and debt management is necessary to prevent mistakes impelling the economy toward inflation or depression. Prevention is far easier than cure.

In considering the measures to correct or prevent unemployment and inflation, it is vital not to lose sight of long-run forces. Management of aggregate demand through the proper use of monetary and fiscal policy is not the only requisite of proper macroeconomic policy. Account must also be taken of the companion management of supply. In the long run supply management is even more important than demand management.

I have said very little so far about aggregate supply and supply management. The latter involves, first and foremost, those factors affecting the aggregate supply of commodities at given prices. An excessive increase in wage rates as a result of wage settlements in excess of increases in productivity will increase costs of production and reduce aggregate supply at any given level of prices. Without an increase in prices (which would reduce the commodity value of the wage settlements), some workers will then be left unemployed. To prevent unemployment, prices will have to increase, and they will increase sufficiently to avoid unemployment only if there is a corresponding increase in demand, which in turn will come about only if there is an increase in liquidity. There is therefore great pressure on the central bank and the government to respond to inflationary wage increases by increasing liquidity, "ratifying" the inflationary wage settlement.

This *cost-push* process is a familiar feature of modern economies. An initial disequilibrium caused by an excessive increase in money wages raises prices and causes some unemployment, which the authorities prevent by increasing effective demand through more expansive monetary and fiscal policy. Prices rise sufficiently to restore the initial commodity value of wages (so-called efficiency wages), but labor unions again react by demanding higher wages, which causes higher prices, more money, and still higher prices and wages. The secular wage creep—technically a series of wage increases in excess of the productivity of the last unit of labor hired—places the government in a particularly difficult position. If, on the one hand, it does not expand demand, unemployment and unused capacity will result, whereas if it prevents the unemployment by more expansive policies, it contributes to inflation. In the short run all the arguments are for expanding demand; in the long run restraint and control over the disturbing sector of the economy are necessary. To this end the government often attempts to persuade or control indirectly the activities of the disturbing element, as in the case of the wage guidelines exhorting unions to ask for no more than the secular increase in productivity of the economy. The wage-guidelines policy was an attempt to solve a dilemma of the modern economy: how to preserve a high level of employment without causing inflation.

The phrase "high level of employment" has to be interpreted with caution. Most people of common sense recognize that excess capacity is a great waste. This was certainly the case in the 1930s, when huge quantities of capital equipment and labor resources were left idle. But care must be exercised in deciding what excess capacity is. There is excess capacity in your home when you are not in it and on the streets when they are not being used. There is excess capacity in a theater after closing hours, in a radio when it is not turned on, in a suit of clothes or a dress you are not using, in a painting you are not looking at, in an empty park, and on high seas. One of the major problems in economics is to decide at what rate to use things, which involves the problem of determining how we should measure excess capacity.

There is always a certain amount of unused capacity in the economy. Capital-goods and labor resources can never be utilized 100 percent over any extended period of time. Full employment does not mean that every worker has a job, since some are necessarily in the process of changing jobs. It does not mean that every worker who wants a job can have one at any conceivable wage rate, since the possibility of his being employed depends on the relation between his wage and his productivity. It is in a restricted sense of excess supply rather than simply in the sense of idle capacity that the problem of unemployment must be understood.

Governments usually have to strike a balance in the management of the economy between policies that stimulate demand and policies that affect supply. It is only rarely that they can achieve an optimum utilization of the labor force and the capital stock of an economy and at the same time attain other goals of economic policy such as the appropriate rate of economic growth, the desired degree of price stability, and the appropriate composition of the balance of payments.

12. *Classicists and Romanticists*

Economics has been called the gloomy science, no doubt because three economists in the nineteenth century, Ricardo, Malthus, and Marx, preached doctrines that were hardly a cause for glee: Ricardo, that wages equaled bare subsistence and not much *could* be done about it; Malthus, that population outran the food supply and not much *would* be done about it; and Marx, that the capitalist system was going to break down anyway and not much *should* be done about it.

There is, however, a sense in which economics has to be gloomy. It is much more fun to match resources to aims than to have to reduce aims to fit resources; to make opportunities to satisfy desires than to restrain desires within opportunities; and to match incomes to spending plans rather than to trim expenditure to a given income.

It is much more fun, but it is not always feasible. The traditional role of the classical economist has been the cautious and conservative one of reiterating that consumption cannot exceed production and that any increase in the share received by one sector of the economy implies a decrease in the share of other sectors. To achieve given spending goals, any sector of an economy must have the means of financing them. The spirit of the classical tradition in economics was that consumption must be budgeted to the style of living that production can support.

In the 1930s, however, there developed another tradition. Born of the Great Depression, this tradition was romantic in spirit.

The spirit of this approach was not to adapt expenditure to income, but to manage expenditure in such a way as to produce maximum income. This is what the Keynesian revolution was about.

To see the significance of the change in emphasis from the classical to the romantic tradition, it is necessary to see how the Keynesians overturned, to their satisfaction, the classical proposition "Supply creates its own demand." The meaning of this proposition is that the production of a good itself involves payment to the factors engaged in production—payments in the form of rents, wages, and interest. These payments represent incomes out of which additional spending will result. An increase in supply, therefore, creates additional incomes for the factors of production, and this additional income brings about an increased demand for commodities. Thus supply creates its own demand and a general excess of supply over demand is impossible. There may be an excess of supply over demand for particular products, but there cannot be an excess supply (a glut) of all goods in the aggregate, since for every excess supply in one market there will be an equal excess demand in the aggregate of other markets. The proposition has come to be called *Say's law* or *Walras's law*, depending, as we shall see, on how it is interpreted.

Whether this proposition is a general law or not depends on the meaning attached to "excess supply." If "excess supply" applies to *all* things, *including money*, then it is true at all points in time, since demand implies an offer of money in exchange, and supply implies a demand for money in exchange; on this interpretation the proposition is called Walras's law and is true at all points of time. But if "excess supply" refers only to commodities, *and money is not counted as a commodity*, then the proposition that supply creates its own demand implies the impossibility of an excess demand for money; on this interpretation the proposition is called Say's law, and it is not true at all moments of time, but only when cash balances are in equilibrium.

What did the classical economists mean when they said there could be no excess supply in the aggregate? Did they mean to include or exclude money? John Stuart Mill, whom Keynes singled out as typical of the economists representing the "erroneous" classical view, wrote:

> First, let us suppose that the quantity of commodities produced is not greater than the community would be glad to consume: is it, in that case, possible that there should be a deficiency of demand for all commodities for want of the means of payment? Those who think so cannot have considered what it is which constitutes the means of payment for commodities. It is simply commodities. Each person's means of paying for the productions of other people consist of those which he himself possesses. All sellers are inevitably and *ex vi termini* buyers. Could we suddenly double the productive powers of the country, we should double the supply of commodities in every market; but we should, by the same stroke, double the purchasing power. Everybody would bring a double demand as well as supply: everybody would be able to buy twice as much, because everyone would have twice as much to offer in exchange. It is probable, indeed, that there would now be a superfluity of certain things. Although the community would willingly double its aggregate consumption, it may already have as much as it desires of some commodities, and it may prefer to do more than double its consumption of others, or to exercise its increased purchasing power on some new thing. If so, the supply will adapt itself accordingly, and the value of things will continue to conform to their costs of production. At any rate it is sheer absurdity that all things should fall in value, and that all producers should, in consequence, be insufficiently remunerated. If values remain the same, what becomes of prices is immaterial, since the remuneration of producers does not depend on how much money, but on how much consumable articles they obtain for their goods. *Besides,*

> *money is a commodity;* and if all commodities are supposed to be doubled in quantity, we must suppose money to be doubled too, and then prices would no more fall than values would.*

From this passage it is clear enough that Mill intended "excess supply of all commodities" to be interpreted to include money. In this sense no economist has ever denied the proposition. However, Keynes, attacking Mill's proposition, which he quoted, left out the last half of the paragraph shown above in which Mill made his meaning explicit.† Whether this omission was by design or carelessness is not clear. What is evident, however, is that Keynes perpetrated a historical error in the economics profession lasting several years, a distortion of the classical position that to this day remains in the elementary textbooks. By thus attacking the logic of a central feature of the classical theory through carelessness or mischievous omission of its essential parts, Keynes was able to win disciples over to the belief that there was a fatal logical defect, an absurd premise, in the classical system. The classicists were guilty, according to Keynes, of believing in Say's law, and could not develop a theory of the fluctuations of output as a whole. In place of the classical emphasis on the proposition that supply creates its own demand, Keynes came very close to a new dictum, that demand creates its own supply. It is just as true to say that Keynes propagated the belief that demand would get supplied as it is to say that the classicists believed that supply would get demanded.

The practical implications of the newly developed romantic tradition were that all sectors in the economy (households, businesses, and governments) could increase their spending at the same time and that under certain circumstances supply would adapt to the increase in demand, and inflationary pres-

* John Stuart Mill, *Principles of Political Economy*, 1909, pp. 557–558.
† J. M. Keynes, *The General Theory of Employment, Interest and Money*, 1936, p. 18.

sures would not develop. By contrast, the classical theory implied that one sector of an economy could increase its spending, in real terms, only at the expense of spending in other sectors.

The major theoretical issues raised by Keynes have now been resolved. In depression, when there are unutilized resources and money wage rates are "sticky downward," aggregate demand for commodities can be increased in relation to aggregate supply; and since an increase in supply can be encouraged with relatively little inflation, real income will increase as a result. But in periods when the labor force and businesses are working at peak capacity, aggregate supply cannot be increased, and demand must be restrained to available supply; if it were not, inflation would result. In short, during periods of depression we can afford to be romanticists, since all sectors can spend and consume more at the same time, whereas during inflationary periods we must be classicists, since one sector's spending can only be increased in real terms at the expense of the spending of other sectors of the economy.

The main policy variables that can be used to alter aggregate demand are, as we saw in the last chapter, monetary policy (changes in the money supply or interest rates) and fiscal policy (changes in the level of government spending or taxation). The main factors affecting aggregate supply are wage rates and productivity. Experience has shown that measures affecting both aggregate demand and aggregate supply are necessary if a high level of utilization of resources and a reasonably stable price level are to be achieved.

In the short run demand management is more important. During depression the government, in the interests of full employment, can move in the direction of more spending, lower taxes, and easy monetary conditions to increase aggregate demand.

During inflationary periods, on the other hand, the government can move in the direction of higher taxes, lower government spending, and tighter money-market conditions to decrease aggregate demand, to prevent inflation.

As we saw in Chapter 11, however, measures that rely solely on demand management suffer from an inherent defect. If not used in cooperation with supply management, they can lead in the long run to inflation. This is especially true if there is persistent upward pressure on wage rates over and above natural increases justified by improvements in the productivity of the labor force. Demand-management policies would lead to secular inflation if wage bargains were continually being struck in advance of productivity gains. The need to exert some sort of control over wages and other costs—supply management—is rendered more important when we come to consider balance-of-payments problems in connection with stabilization policy. Not only does macroeconomic policy have to try to achieve full employment and price stability; it must also deal with the problem of preserving a balance-of-payments equilibrium.

The balance-of-payments accounts can be divided roughly into two parts. One part, the current account, measures the difference between current sales of goods and services to foreigners and purchases from them. In equilibrium the excess of what is bought from foreigners over what is sold to foreigners must be matched by net borrowing from them. For the United States, which typically sells more goods to foreigners than it purchases, it is clearer to express this equilibrium as a balance between net sales abroad and net lending (including foreign aid).

Here we see the restraining hand of classical economics. If Americans pay out money to foreigners in (net) loans or gifts and receive money from foreigners by selling abroad more than they purchase abroad, the United States balance-of-payments accounts are in equilibrium. But if they lend (or give) more than the current-account balance, foreigners will acquire extra dollars that can be cashed in for United States gold. If this process went on for a long time, the United States Treasury would run out of gold.

One qualification is necessary, however, because the United

States occupies a very special position at the center of the international monetary system; it is in one sense a banker's banker. Foreign central banks—the Bank of Canada, the Banque de France, the Bundesbank, the Banca d'Italia, and so on—keep their reserves not in gold alone, as the United States very nearly does, but also partly in dollars, which can be cashed in for gold at the United States Treasury. Since 1945, when the dollar was absolute king, these countries wanted to build up their dollar holdings (which were cashable into gold but nevertheless earned interest), and so they ran surpluses with the United States, financed by huge United States gifts and loans through the Marshall Plan; the United States ran deficits, which averaged, between 1945 and 1958, about $1 billion a year. These were sustainable, since the foreign banks placed the dollars in their New York accounts rather than cashing them for gold, as Europe especially needed to rebuild its stocks of foreign exchange.

But the situation changed abruptly, about 1958. The European countries had recovered completely from the war, grown at a tremendous pace, formed the Common Market, and established the convertibility of their own currencies. Their increased competitiveness, combined with the 1949 and 1958 devaluations of their currencies, contributed to a slowing down of the growth of United States exports and an increase in United States imports. These factors were combined with a continuation of United States foreign aid, and, most important, a capital movement to Europe as American companies tried to get in on the ground floor of the vast new Common Market. This meant that the gap between United States net sales and net lending widened, and the United States deficit jumped from about $1 billion a year to $3 billion a year.

But the central banks in the rest of the world did not want to accumulate $3 billion in dollar holdings a year; they only wanted about $1 billion. The difference began to be taken out in gold at a rate of close to $1 billion a year. It would have been higher, except that many of the central banks in countries that were the beneficiaries of postwar United States aid were reluctant to embarrass the United States. At any rate, the United States gold stock was over $22 billion in 1957, but by 1967 it had dwindled to less than $13 billion, United States liquid liabilities having jumped over the same period from about $9 billion to $17 billion. The two of these together, the gold loss and the increase in liabilities, from 1957 to 1967 totaled over $17 billion, a figure which represents one measure of the accumulated United States balance-of-payments deficit over that period.

Of course $13 billion still seems like a lot of gold that could last, at the current rate of gold loss, for another decade. But this understates the gravity of the problem, not because gold is needed to back United States currency (it is, but the law could easily be changed again as it was in 1965), but because the threat of future gold loss feeds speculation about the price of gold. If foreign monetary authorities began to believe, as many private speculators now believe, that the price of gold might be increased, there might, failing a monetary agreement, be a cumulative rush to convert all foreign-held dollars into gold. If at any time confidence were to be shaken by an important world event—whether an expansion of the Vietnam war or devaluation of sterling—a cumulative rush to gold could crumble the whole existing fabric and force a devaluation of the dollar. To be sure, most European countries would be exceedingly reluctant to bring this about, but the point is that the existing structure of the system is fragile enough so that it could come about.

The classicist-romanticist dilemma is, therefore, more complicated than it appeared to be when we neglected foreign-trade considerations. In an economy in which foreign trade and balance-of-payments considerations can be neglected, it is enough to say that when there is excess unemployment, an increase in aggregate demand combined with a limitation on increases in wage rates can restore prosperity without inflation; and when there are inflationary pressures and labor shortages, a decrease in aggregate spending combined with a more permissive policy with respect to wages can prevent inflation without causing unemployment. In short we can be policy romanticists during depression and classicists during boom.

But when we take into account the balance of payments and other international considerations, policy making is not that simple. The policies required to restore prosperity during a depression or inflation will differ according to whether gold is flowing in or flowing out. We could in fact just as correctly say that we can be romanticists when gold is flowing in and must be classicists when gold is flowing out.

13. *The Balance of Payments*

It is to a consideration of the balance of payments that we can now turn. The essentials of balance-of-payments problems can be understood by reference to the particular household, as we saw in Chapter 5. We can start off with the proposition that the spending of any household is restrained by liquidity and will be lower or higher in relation to income as liquidity is insufficient or in excess. If a household couple find a sum of cash by chance, they will probably part with most of it in exchange for goods or securities; if they lose a part of their cash holdings, again by chance, they will have to cut back their spending in order to rebuild their reserves.

This is also true of a bank. If a bank loses important customers who ordinarily keep their money on deposit, the bank's cash reserve will go down, and the banker will have to build these back by curtailing new loans or not renewing old ones or by getting new customers. Suppose customers shift their deposits from bank A to bank B, both banks being in the same community. The depositors write checks on bank A and deposit them in bank B, so that after the checks are cleared, B's reserves will have gone up and A's will have gone down by the amount of the checks. Then B has an excess and A a shortage of cash reserves, so that the B-banker will expand his loans and the A-banker will contract his, until the ordinary ratio of reserves to deposits is restored in each bank. The curtailment of loans to A's borrowers encourages them to seek funds elsewhere, while the need to expand loans in B makes the B-banker seek out good credit risks. A new equilibrium will be reached when assets and liabilities in bank B have increased and assets and liabilities in bank A have decreased. Provided the banks have the same reserve ratios, no change in total spending need result, and bank B may simply take over the customers of bank A.

But now suppose banks A and B are in separate communities and that A's borrowers cannot borrow from bank B for some reason (perhaps because both banks make mortgage loans). How will the transfer take place if some of A's customers transfer their money to B?

The first impact, after the checks are cleared, is for A's reserves to go down and B's reserves to go up by the amount of the checks. Bank B looks around for new borrowers, while bank A looks around for borrowers to drop or for new depositors. The B-banker may lower interest rates to attract new borrowers, and the A-banker may raise interest rates to discourage new borrowers or attract new depositors. The easier credit in bank B is conducive to new investment projects and greater expenditure by community B as a whole, while the tighter credit in bank A works in the opposite direction in community A. The greater expenditure on goods in community B will typically be divided between increased demand there for B's own goods and for A's goods, whereas the reduced expenditure on goods in community A will reduce demand there for A's own goods and for B's goods.

The opposing expenditure changes mean that community B will be buying a larger quantity of goods from community A, and A will be buying a smaller quantity of goods from B. To pay for this excess of imports over exports, residents in B will have to write checks on their bank accounts to residents of A, which will be deposited in bank A, thus replenishing the reserves of bank A and mitigating the extent to which the A-banker has to curtail loans to his borrowers, as well as the extent to which the B-banker makes additional advances to his customers.

The process comes to an end when a certain fraction of the initial transfer of deposits has been made in terms of goods—that fraction needed to transfer the reserves to support the switch of deposits. Suppose, for example, that the initial transfer of deposits amounted to $1,000 and that both bankers keep 10 percent of their deposit liabilities in currency reserves. Then, after the expansion of loans in community B and the contraction of loans in community A, $100 in goods over a space of time will have to be transferred from A to B, after which the two communities will be again in the original position except for the additional accounts some A residents hold in bank B and the additional stock of goods accumulated by B residents. In the course of the transfer some prices may have changed, of course.

This transfer process is so important in international economics that it is well to put it in an even simpler context. Suppose I have to pay you a dollar, and do so. The dollar you get permits your total spending to rise by about that amount (unless you want to increase your liquidity), and the dollar I have given up makes me reduce my total spending by a dollar (unless I want to decrease my liquidity). In the course of your using the dollar your spending will exceed your income by a dollar, and mine will fall short of my income by a dollar. The dollar will then come back to me from you, while goods will have moved from me, through the market, to you. The financial transfer has to have a counterpart in goods or net borrowings after the original liquidity position is restored. The same process that occurs between individuals also applies to communities, and it is only complicated—it is not changed in principle—when there are banks.

Let us now expand our concept by imagining that A and B represent separate communities with several banks in each.

None of the principles of transfer are altered. A transfer of money from a bank in A to a bank in B will induce a movement of goods by an amount depending on the reserve ratios of banks in A and B. In effect the transfers will involve the acquisition by A residents of a claim on banks in B, which requires a shift of reserves, which are "bought" by shipping goods to B.

But let us now introduce separate currencies for communities A and B. Suppose community A uses dollars and community B pounds sterling, both of which are convertible into gold. This was indeed the situation prevailing between America and Britain before 1914 and between 1925 and 1931, when both Britain and America were on the gold standard, the ratio of the gold content of the pound to the gold content of the dollar being 4.867 and the exchange rate, or price of the pound in terms of the dollar, being $4.867 = £1.

Let us suppose, then, that some Americans (community A) want to transfer a balance to a bank in Britain (community B) of, say, £1,000 ($4,867). They write a check on their joint account in an American bank for $4,867 and send the check to the British bank. Their deposits at the American bank go down by $4,867, and their deposits at the British bank go up by £1,000, so they have achieved what they want by the transfer.

But the process does not end here. Since the British bank will want pounds or gold, not dollars, it will send the check drawn on the American bank for "clearance." Since the American bank commits itself to keep its deposits convertible into gold, the British bank will ask for the equivalent in gold from the American bank. The American bank will then honor the check by shipping an equivalent in gold from its reserves to the British bank. Thus the gold reserves of the American bank will go down and the gold reserves of the British bank will go up by an equivalent amount. The British bank is now liquid because while its deposit liabilities have gone up by £1,000, it has an additional £1,000 worth of gold, and it only needs to keep a fraction of gold reserves backing its deposits. Similarly, the American bank is now illiquid because while its deposit liabilities have gone down by $4,867, its gold reserves have gone down by the same amount; and since it too keeps only a fraction of gold reserves behind deposits, the ratio of gold to deposits has gone down.

Because it is liquid, the British bank will seek profitable investments (loans) in which to place its excess reserves and in the process of encouraging borrowing will perhaps lower interest rates somewhat, while the American bank will cut back on new loans and even be willing to sell some treasury bills. To protect its earnings, the British bank may buy up some liquid assets, perhaps even the same United States bills the American bank has tried to sell. But to some extent the tighter market conditions in the United States will reduce bank lending and private spending, while the easier market conditions in Britain will increase bank lending and private spending. Americans will spend less, the British will spend more, and the transfer will be effected in terms of goods (or loans) in the same way as in our simpler example. The existence of different currencies thus does not alter the basic process, even though it complicates its exposition. America will initially have a balance-of-payments deficit and Britain a surplus that will be reflected in the gold flow between the two countries. Yet this gold flow itself sets in motion self-correcting forces. Through expenditure changes in each country and an improvement in the balance of trade (the difference between exports and imports), the financial transfer of money is effected in part (equal to the needed redistribution of gold reserves) in real terms. Further complications could be introduced by allowing for the cost of shipping gold (including insurance) and the small fluctuations in the exchange rate to which this cost gives rise, but these are mere details that would only complicate the exposition without altering its substance.

But suppose we now go one step further and assume that except for pocket cash, ordinary members of the American and British communities keep their money reserves in banks, that banks, except for cash in the till, keep their reserves in the central bank, and that the two central banks keep their reserves in gold. Deposits are convertible into currencies and currencies are convertible into gold. Is the transfer principle altered in any important respect?

The answer again is no, provided the central banks allow the gold-standard adjustment mechanism to operate. Instead of shipping its own gold (which it does not have) to a London bank, the American commercial bank will have to take some of its currency reserves and buy the gold from its central bank to ship to the London bank; and the London bank will in turn sell the gold to the Bank of England, getting deposits or currency from the Bank of England in exchange. The reserves of the Federal Reserve go down and those of the Bank of England go up by the amount of the transfer. If the central banks keep all their currency backed by gold (as the Swiss central bank currently does), the currency supply outstanding in England will go up and that outstanding in the United States will go down by the amount of the transfer, and the same process of adjustment will take place as in the preceding example, starting off with excess bank reserves in Britain and a shortage of bank reserves in the United States.

We are now getting very close to the current system. In the nineteenth century London was the center of the world's financial system, with the Bank of England first among the central banks. But the world wars weakened Britain as a financial power, and the financial center of the world shifted from London toward New York for certain important functions. After the Second World War other central banks began to hold their reserves not in gold alone but also in dollar deposits in New York; and they kept their currencies convertible, after postwar recovery, into dollars instead of gold. Only the United States kept the dollar convertible into gold, and then not for its own citizens or banks, but only for foreign central banks for what was judged to be legitimate monetary purposes. The dollar at the end of the war and up to 1960 stood side by side with gold as an international reserve.

In Chapter 15 we shall examine some of the implications of having a national currency like the dollar behave as an international money and some of the problems this has created since 1960. But at the moment our concern is with the process of international adjustment to the balance of payments.

The process of adjustment altered in the course of the movement away from the gold standard. After the Second World War countries increasingly adopted a practice, begun by the Federal Reserve in the 1920s, of adjusting the domestic supply of money to maintain the correct level of aggregate demand for preventing inflation or unemployment. (The governments of major countries had failed miserably in preventing unemployment in the interwar period). This meant a gradual change from the automatic adjustment process that existed under the gold standard toward a process in which balances of payments are allowed to be in disequilibrium for long periods of time. Let us see the implications of this change in policy.

Suppose we have, as before, our American and British central banks keeping gold as backing for their currencies. Under the old process, when Americans transferred money from United States banks to British banks, enough gold moved from America to Britain to support the higher deposits in Britain, and then the gold flow ceased.

But the new process of using the supply of money to achieve domestic objectives ruptures this adjustment process. When the United States loses gold, the money supply initially goes down, and money-market conditions become tighter. To prevent a tightening in the money market, the central bank buys an amount of government securities equal to the amount of gold lost; this keeps the money supply from going down and forestalls any danger the authorities may see of deflation. Similarly, in Britain, the Bank of England prevents the influx of gold from easing money-market conditions and increasing demand in that country, to prevent the danger, which it expects, of inflation.

But here is the rub. Whatever the advantages of this policy of sterilizing the monetary effects of balance-of-payments disequilibrium may have been for domestic purposes, it perpetuates the balance-of-payments disturbance in that it creates a balance-of-payments problem that hitherto did not exist. When the United States authorities sterilize the gold flow by buying bonds, more purchasing power is created, and United States spending increases; United States residents, who had decided to hold fewer dollars and more pounds than before, now find the dollars they willingly parted with replenished by the central bank, which, in effect, creates credit for the community to spend. Accordingly Americans spend the excess dollars either on home or foreign goods (or more typically both), creating a balance-of-payments deficit. This deficit itself causes a gold outflow and the needed reduction in the money supply, but again the Federal Reserve does not allow the community to reduce its money balances; it merely sterilizes the gold flow again by more purchases of government bonds, which perpetuates the disequilibrium and increases the gold loss.

The process is aggravated by a similar policy in Britain, which will not allow the money supply in Britain to rise by the amount of the new balances Americans want to hold there. The Bank of England (or, more exactly, the Exchange Equalization Account) sells government bonds every time it gains gold and thus prevents the expansion of sterling needed in Britain to satisfy the increased demand for sterling balances. The British practice, like the American, helps to perpetuate the disequilibrium and allows balance-of-payments problems to persist until gold flows force a change in policy or a devaluation of the weak currency.

The working of this system is only slightly altered by taking into account the fact that the Bank of England keeps the pound fixed in terms of dollars rather than gold and maintains working dollar balances in New York. Let us make, however, the slight transition because it fits the present institutional context.

When the dollars are transferred to London, British banks sell the dollars for pounds, and, following the law of supply and demand, the price of the pound tends to rise in terms of dollars. The parity of the pound expressed in dollars is fixed at \$2.80 = £1 (since the 1949 devaluation of the pound), but support points are \$2.78 and \$2.82, which means as we saw in Chapter 8, that the Bank of England will intervene in the market by selling dollars (losing reserves) when the pound drops to \$2.78 and by buying dollars (gaining reserves) when the pound rises to \$2.82; the central bank may also intervene in between these limits. Suppose, then, that the pound rises to \$2.82; the Bank of England steps in and buys up the excess dollars (adding them to the New York account), selling pounds in exchange. But to prevent the supply of pounds in British banks from increasing, the Bank of England automatically sells government bonds (or other domestic financial assets), mopping up the excess pounds. The Bank of England then converts the dollars it has acquired into gold at the United States Treasury, and everything is the same as before.

A disequilibrium system of this kind, which is justified by the authorities of each country on the grounds that they need to follow an "independent" national monetary policy, prevents balances of payments from being equilibrated. As we shall see in Chapter 15, this practice is an unsound one, but it is complicated by the special role played by the United States in the world's monetary system.

14. *Internal and External Balance*

We return now to the problem of correcting the United States balance-of-payments deficit while at the same time preserving full employment without inflation. To see how these goals are related to one another and also to illustrate the importance of the choice between monetary and fiscal policy in restraining inflation at the present time, let us go back to the Kennedy years to see how the United States got into its present position.

When Kennedy came to power in 1961, there was excess unemployment, slow economic growth, and a nagging balance-of-payments deficit. Remember now that when there is considerable unemployment, we can be romanticists rather than classicists, since everybody can spend more without causing much inflation. Good classicists would want to lower money wages (or prevent money wages from rising rapidly), but not much hope was held out for that policy in the short run; guidelines policy was to be a "long-run policy."

Now granted that we want to stimulate demand, how can we achieve the stimulus? Clearly by an expansive fiscal policy (lower taxes or more government spending) or an expansive monetary policy (lower interest rates or a more rapid rate of monetary expansion).

If there were no balance-of-payments problem to consider, the decision between expansive monetary policy and expansive fiscal policy would not be such a crucial decision, and we would probably settle for a combination of both policies, leaning slightly toward expansive monetary policy since budget deficits can have an unfavorable effect on long-run growth. But when there is a balance-of-payments deficit, there is this problem: Any expansion of domestic demand, at given interest rates, will aggravate the balance-of-payments deficit. This is true regardless of whether the stimulus comes from monetary policy or from fiscal policy.

There is, however, one basic difference when we take into account the balance of payments. When capital is mobile between countries, it is likely to move to where interest rates are higher, so that any policy that stimulates demand while raising interest rates will have less of a worsening effect on the balance of payments than one that achieves the same level of demand goal while decreasing interest rates.

This provides the key to the solution. Because there was a deficit in the balance of payments in the early sixties, the best way to stimulate demand was by fiscal policy. A tax reduction would stimulate demand, put pressure on the credit markets, and lift interest rates along with the expansion of national income; it would also reduce the outflow of capital to foreign countries and thus dampen the adverse effect on (and perhaps even improve) the balance of payments. It would be a short-run solution because it would cut down lending and alter the mix between consumption and investment, but at that time the unemployment problem was a short-run problem. The policy mix could be useful while a less expansionary wage policy was being introduced.

The choice of this policy mix was confirmed after a speech Kennedy made to the New York Economic Club at the end of 1962, and the tax reduction was introduced the following year. The economy, partly on its own momentum and partly as a result of this stimulus, moved forward to new levels of productivity, to more rapid growth, and to a high level of employment, and, also, the balance of payments seemed to get a little better.

Everything worked fine up until 1965. Then the policy began to work too well. The authorities miscalculated when they failed to take into account the rapid increase in military spending occasioned by the Vietnam war. Unemployment fell in early 1966 to about 3.7 percent, but prices began to rise. The war added a stimulus equal again to the tax cut; the combined effect of the two helped push the economy past the brink of safety into inflation. Fiscal policy could not have done this alone.

The tax cut and the increase in military spending that was superimposed on the domestic boom would have caused a rise in interest rates (remember a policy of tighter money was to be one of the safeguards for the balance of payments). But the Federal Reserve stepped in with a more rapid rate of monetary expansion, pressured by the administration to prevent interest rates from rising rapidly. You may remember 1965 as a year of tightness in the money market.* It is true that interest rates were rising, but it is also true that the rate of monetary expansion was rapid enough to stimulate an inflationary expansion of spending.

The late spring and early summer of 1966 aroused considerable controversy among policy makers and economists. There was a

* When is money easy, and when is it tight? One answer is that money is easy when interest rates are low or falling and that it is tight when interest rates are high or rising; another answer is that money is easy when the rate of monetary expansion is high or increasing and that it is tight when the rate of monetary expansion is low or decreasing. Old-fashioned Keynesians use the former criteria, while old-fashioned classicists use the latter. Most modern economists, on the other hand, like to look at all measures and take account of the cyclical pattern of movements of interest rates and the rate of monetary expansion. In theory, of course, the fluctuations in the rate of interest are an unreliable test of the tightness or ease of monetary policy because the return to capital (real profit rates) fluctuates with the business cycle, rising and falling as the ratio of employed labor to utilized equipment increases and decreases.

balance-of-payments deficit accompanied by inflationary pressure, fed by a rapid rate of monetary expansion that was trying to finance too much of the budget deficit that was growing out of the escalation of the war in Vietnam. Tightening of either monetary or fiscal policy would help to restrain the inflation and at the same time reduce the balance-of-payments deficit. Tight money would do it mainly at the expense of investment, higher taxes more at the expense of consumption. The main problem was to restrain demand and thus stop the inflation without toppling the economy into a recession.

The key question in the middle of 1966 was to recognize that a mistake had been made in the preceding year. Taxes should have been increased substantially in early 1966 to finance the Vietnam war, but they were not. In the absence of action by the Treasury, the Federal Reserve had to step in and bear the whole of the burden of reducing demand. Starting in the middle of 1966, it turned off the monetary tap and introduced the greatest United States credit squeeze in decades—a squeeze that, because of the great size of the United States, had ramifications all over the world. Interest rates shot up in the face of an excess demand for credit, and inflationary pressures were contained.

It should not be thought, however, that the apparent success of the credit squeeze of 1966 vindicated the government's policy. The squeeze drastically reduced demand but, along with the budget deficit of the government, left the economy in a distorted position and hurt particular sectors like housing. Also, the inflation of 1965 and early 1966 had set in motion wage expectations likely to cause trouble later on.

The problem of expectations—one of the dimensions of confidence—creates a major difficulty for policy in the long run. The inflationary pressures in years such as 1965 and early 1966 affect judgments about future prices. Insofar as consumers and investors anticipate inflation in the future, they go on spending and investing and are not worried so much about rising interest rates. Interest rates in 1965 and 1966 *appeared* high, but if you look closely you will see that, in real terms, the appearance was deceiving. After all, if a one-year bond yields 5 percent and prices are rising by 3 percent, the debt is repaid in depreciated money, so that the *real* interest being paid is only 2 percent. There are all kinds of profitable investments on which business can earn, after risk and taxes, three or four times that return on capital. The real interest rate was too low for stability, and that has the effect of overextending investment in particular industries.

As suggested above, a second factor in the expectations process is wages. Wages and productivity have both risen fairly steadily in most countries over the postwar period. But an acceleration of inflation means that the *real* wage has not risen as fast as it otherwise would, and this is a factor, once management-labor bargains have been struck, that reduces unemployment or causes a labor scarcity, and raises profits.

In the early stages of inflation these two things happen: First, money interest rates rise but do not compensate fully for the inflation, so that *real* interest rates fall, a factor that gives a great stimulus to profits and investment; second, money wage rates rise with productivity, but *efficiency* wage rates (wage rates in relation to productivity) fall in real terms, another factor increasing profits and investment, and feeding the boom.

Both these forces create pressures for additional expansion. But they do not last. Eventually money wages catch up as cost-of-living compensation gets built into wage contracts, and money interest rates catch up as increasing tightness in the capital market builds an inflation premium into the interest-rate structure. Then money wages catch up to efficiency wages and may overshoot, and money interest catches up to real interest and may overshoot, either or both of which together can bring on a collapse of demand and a recession. Inflation breeds expectations which are not realizable in the long run and introduces fundamental long-run problems for wage policy.

Some of these problems can be put in the more general context of the recently developed theory of economic policy.

No target (a goal of policy) can be achieved without an instrument (a means of implementing policy).

A guidelines policy in which the government suggests that wages rise by no more than a given rate depends for its success on the effect of the guidelines on supply of and demand for labor. A union can enforce a given wage in the labor market only if it possesses the instrument to alter the supply of, and demand for, labor. Union members may agree to set a wage and to work for no less than that wage. Employers have to accept the wage, but still supply is equal to demand, since firms hire only that quantity of labor they want. In this case the instrument by which the wage rate is maintained is the agreement among the workers and the willingness of the union to allow some members to go without jobs.

One instrument that is widely used to achieve higher wages is minimum legal wage rates. It is often thought that this policy cannot affect real wages, but this rests on a misconception. Minimum wage rates that are effective, in the sense that some workers previously got less than the minimum wage, can raise wages by altering the supply of, and demand for, other types of labor. A law-abiding firm that previously hired low-wage workers will now demand no workers below the minimum wage, so that all workers will be paid the minimum wage rate or more. Firms will not hire workers whose productivity is less than the minimum wage, but will substitute workers whose productivity is higher and machines that can do the work previously done by those workers who are now unemployed. The demand for high-productivity workers whose type of work is competitive with that of the low-productivity workers will rise, and their wage rates will rise.

Now if the government, recognizing the increased unemployment of those cut off by the minimum wage, expanded the money supply, thus raising prices to lower the commodity value of the real wage, the original position of full employment could be restored with a higher general money wage rate but the same real wage rate. Thus minimum wage laws may be an instrument for attaining higher real wages provided they cause unemployment of the low-productivity workers; they will leave unaltered the real wage only insofar as employment remains at its original level.

This helps to illustrate the basic principle of the theory of economic policy that an instrument is always necessary to achieve a given target. If full employment is a target of employment policy, there must be an instrument (for example, wage rates) to achieve it; if a given stock of gold reserves is a target of international economic policy, there must be an instrument (for example, monetary policy) to achieve it; if a given role of economic growth is a target of economic policy, there must be an instrument (for example, tax rates) to achieve it.

If there is more than one target, there must be more than one instrument. If two targets can be attained by one instrument, they are misnamed as two targets; they are in fact only one (or else the instrument is misnamed as one instrument). Thus monetary policy alone cannot achieve both balance-of-payments equilibrium and full employment; the two are separate targets, and the level of money needed to hold external reserves constant is different from the level of money needed to achieve full employment for any given money wage rate. But wage rates and monetary policy used together as independent instruments can achieve full employment and balance-of-payments equilibrium.

Monetary policy and wage rates each affect the balance of payments and each affect the level of employment, and there is an equilibrium level of wage rates and an equilibrium level of money that will achieve both targets. But it may not be easy to find out what the equilibrium values are, and this means that information acquired through trial and error or the freedom of the market will have to be exploited. The question then arises whether one instrument is in any way specially related to a particular target. Should wage rates be adjusted to employment and the money supply be adjusted to the balance of payments, or should the opposite assignment of instruments and targets be used? The problem thus becomes one in the dynamics of adjustment under conditions of limited information.

One principle that can be applied here is *the principle of effective market classification,* which is a sort of comparative-advantage principle applied to the dynamics of policies. *Instruments should be assigned to the targets they most strongly influence,* or have a comparative advantage in, as it were. Now since the supply of currency itself represents one of the components of the demand for, and supply of, currency as against gold and since the wage rate is itself the price of labor, it follows that the supply of money should be adjusted to equilibrate the balance of payments and that the wage rate should be used to achieve equilibrium between the voluntary supply of, and demand for, labor.*

* The principle of effective market classification applies anywhere at all; thus it has applications in many different fields of science. Assume that to kill two diseases in a patient, two medicines (perhaps antibiotics) must be used. (To kill three diseases, three medicines are required, and so on.) If the two medicines affect each of the diseases but the proper dosage is not known, the principle can be used to determine the proper dosage. Thus if drug A improves disease X but worsens disease Y and drug B improves disease Y but worsens disease X, but the beneficial effect of drug A on X exceeds its harmful effect on Y by a greater proportion than the harmful effect of drug B on X exceeds its beneficial effect on Y, a prescription by which the dosage of A is always increased when X gets worse and the dosage of B is always increased when Y gets worse will always result in a movement toward the equilibrium dose. The opposite assignment would lead away from equilibrium.

The principles of economic policy have general application. To reach a given goal, there must be at least one instrument; if there is more than one instrument, there is more than one way of reaching the goal. If there is more than one target, one instrument cannot achieve it; the number of instruments must be at least as great as the number of targets. And if that is so, the principle of effective market classification can provide information about the dynamic means by which targets can be reached.

Further applications of the theory of policy, relevant to some of the issues we have considered in connection with the balance of payments, can be made in judging the policies of various governments in certain fields over the past few years. These applications are made, of course, with knowledge we now possess that was not known at the time.

Take as an early example the United Kingdom's sterling crisis of 1947, when the British authorities, in the face of diplomatic pressure from the United States and implicit commitments made during the negotiations for the 1946 British loan from the United States, attempted to make the pound sterling convertible. In other words, the British attempted to remove exchange controls. The consequences were disastrous, and the British lost thereby many prior benefits the loan had conferred on them. The mistake in 1947 was to attempt convertibility (by abandoning controls) when there was excessive domestic liquidity and suppressed inflationary pressure, leading to a result which, from the vantage point of modern theory, could have been predicted in advance. Sterling, previously dammed in by exchange controls, flowed into the Bank of England while dollars flowed out. Monetary deflation was needed before convertibility could work. The money supply, in a country that fixes its exchange rate, is the most important determinant of the balance of payments.

A second example, again from Britain. In 1949, in the face of excessive liquidity and inflationary pressure, sterling was devalued. This aggravated the inflationary pressure and led to wage expectations that have plagued the British work force to this day. Devaluation was recognized as a mistake at the time by a few British economists, notably Hawtrey and Harrod,* but more general agreement might be found today. The British policy of devaluation of 1949 offends against the prescription, widely recognized today, that a balance-of-payments deficit combined with excessive inflationary pressure requires monetary restraint (since this operates both to relieve the domestic situation and to preserve foreign-exchange reserves).†

A third example can be taken from Canadian experience from 1958 to 1960, when the Canadian authorities, who had been operating a flexible exchange-rate system since 1950, tightened domestic liquidity by means of a mass conversion-loan (converting short-term debt into long-term debt), raising interest rates; at the same time government expenditure policies increased the budget deficit. The announced *purpose* of the monetary policy was to reduce Canadian spending and thus (!) external borrowing, while the object of the increase in the budgetary deficit was to reduce unemployment. But the *consequence* of the combined policy was to aggravate the current-account deficit without correcting unemployment, as govern-

* When conservatives and liberals agree on policy, authorities should sit up and take notice!

† The issue is a complicated one, however, and it would be unfair to the subtlety of the reasoning of those urging devaluation at the time to dismiss it as a policy wholly at variance with theoretical reasoning. Devaluation had substantial effects on the internal distribution of income and on the real cost of external sterling liabilities, effects which it may have been a purpose of British policy to promote. It is probably more correct, however, to say that devaluation was advanced as a British hedge against the possibility of a world depression inaugurated by the United States recession of 1949. Remarkable as such an interpretation may seem, it is necessary to remember that Keynesian economists in the late 1940s were still worried about a great postwar depression long after Keynes himself, as early as 1945, had become convinced of the dangers of postwar inflation.

ment borrowing bid up interest rates, attracted foreign capital, appreciated the value of the Canadian dollar relative to the United States dollar, and worsened the trade balance. The policy mix was wrong; the appropriate policy in a situation of unemployment, in the context of a flexible exchange system, is monetary ease, which is needed to allow the exchange rate to depreciate, and thus increase exports relative to imports.

A fourth example is offered by Italy. In the early part of 1963, bundles of bank notes amounting to over $1 billion worth of lire were shipped out of Italy as a consequence of uncertainties about the socialist policies being pursued by the Fanfani government. After a Cabinet crisis in August of that year the government was paralyzed, leaving a political vacuum that enabled the Banca d'Italia to take action against the mounting balance-of-payments deficit. The theory—monetary deflation—was correct. But money was tightened by cutting off the access of the commercial banks to the international short-term capital market! The deficit aroused world financial opinion, and the speculative outflow was accelerated. The speculative problem was further aggravated by the indiscretion of an Italian Cabinet member who publicly advocated devaluation. This brought on a crisis, which was reinforced when the Banca d'Italia let the price of lire in the forward exchange market depreciate. Thus official borrowing had to be resorted to instead of the private borrowing that could have continued had the Banca d'Italia adopted a different instrument (for example, higher reserve requirements) for tightening bank liquidity. This example shows how faulty technical execution of an otherwise appropriate policy can bring on a crisis the policy was designed to avoid.

Further examples of mistakes in the face of crises abound on the national level; more interesting, they occur on the level of the international system as well. Thus in 1965 Europe as a whole attempted to control inflation by tighter monetary policy despite heavy budget deficits, while the United States accelerated monetary expansion after the middle of 1965 despite approaching capacity limits and an excessive balance-of-payments deficit (which the monetary policy had helped induce). The upshot was an upward leap in interest rates in Europe and a worsening payments situation, combined with inflationary pressure in the United States. From a world standpoint this was the wrong policy mix; tighter fiscal policy in Europe and tighter monetary policy in the United States were appropriate in the last half of 1965. The reversal of the expansive monetary policy in the United States in the spring of 1966 (a movement toward tight money) caught European countries off balance at a time when some of them, notably Germany and Britain, were threatened by potential recession.

These examples help to illustrate some useful applications of the theory of policy, and also illuminate the defect in our current economic institutions. There is lacking an efficient mechanism for ensuring an appropriate level of aggregate demand in the world as a whole. That gap, as we shall explore in more detail in the next chapter, puts into perspective the need for international monetary reform in a world where many countries outside the United States do not want to keep the present gold-exchange standard based on the dollar.

15. *The Dollar and Gold*

The international monetary system has been in trouble in one way or another for half a century. Prior to 1914 the major nations alternated between gold and silver and bimetallic standards, but since 1870 gold had ruled the roost. Gold was the anonymous monarch in a world of creative nationalism, and it counted for more than a mere medium of exchange and contract; it symbolized internationalism and the rule of international law. Like any sovereign it had its detractors, but these were inconsequential as long as sterling, the power behind the throne, was accorded the respect due the currency of the greatest financial power. National currencies were equal, but sterling was more equal than the others.

The use of a national money as an international reserve asset is not, of course, a new phenomenon; it goes back to Biblical times and was widespread during the Renaissance and the eighteenth century. During the nineteenth century, when the pound sterling was fixed to gold, many central banks outside as well as inside the British Empire held sterling balances in London banks, usually at the Bank of England, to provide a national reserve. The Bank of England, "the Old Lady of Threadneedle Street," managed the system so that when it lost gold, bank rate (the rate charged by the Bank of England on loans) would be raised and a tightness would develop in the London money market, spreading into a general scarcity of liquidity for all those who had stakes in the London capital market.

The London capital market was a world market, with borrowers and lenders placing and taking up loans and capital-market issues through the facilities that the financial center of the empire had developed. When money was scarce in London, it would tend to become scarce all over the world, and a general reduction in world expenditure would take place; when money was easy in London, interest rates all over the world tended to be low. The Bank of England, through its use of bank rate, was the "price leader" in the world monetary system. For a century the bank managed to keep sterling convertible into gold on the basis of an incredibly small gold reserve, by today's standards, relying on confidence in the stability of sterling and the power of London to attract gold through the use of bank rate when it was needed. As Walter Bagehot, the English economist and journalist who wrote *Lombard Street*, said, "8 per cent will bring gold from the moon."

In rough outline, here is how what should probably be called the gold-sterling–exchange standard worked in the world as a whole. Whenever a peripheral country ran short of gold (that is, whenever it had a balance-of-payments deficit), it would allow money-market conditions to tighten (as they would automatically unless the monetary effects of the gold loss were offset by an expansion of domestic credit), thereby attracting capital and curtailing expenditure; and when it had excess gold, it would allow money-market conditions to ease, with the opposite effect. As we have seen, the Bank of England followed the same policy, but since the London capital market was huge in relation to other centers, the Bank of England in effect dominated all others and affected world interest rates and expenditures. Thus whenever the Bank of England was short of gold, world interest rates would be high, and whenever the Bank of England had excess gold, world interest rates would be low. London was the channel through which gold production and hoarding was fed into the world financial system and determined, along with banking operations in the London market, the world price level.

The First World War changed all that. Besides shattering the illusions of a generation brought up to expect continuity and progress as the patrimony of the greatest organized culture the world had ever known, the European "civil war" destroyed the fabric of the international order—an order that was symbolized, in the economic sphere, by the mutual harmony of interests binding trading nations together. The international gold standard broke down completely at the outbreak of war all over the world except the United States, while the agony of the prolonged war and the bitterness it had stamped on an entire generation set the stage for the ill-conceived Treaty of Versailles.

Neither political nor monetary order could be restored on the old basis. America had remained on gold during the war, and on America was laid the heavy responsibility of picking up the pieces. After the war ended, Benjamin Strong, the Governor of the New York Federal Reserve Bank, and Montague Norman, the Governor of the Bank of England (the so-called mystery man of high finance), made valiant attempts to reinstate the old system and spent many fateful hours together reorganizing the currencies of Europe, later joined by Moreau, the Governor of the Bank of France. This team did in the middle twenties what the IMF was to do after the Second World War.

Alas for the welfare of the world, the system had been rebuilt upon sand. Currencies had depreciated in terms of goods, and Britain's fatal error of 1925 (when Churchill was Chancellor of the Exchequer) in going back to the old prewar parity left not only the pound but also the gold base of the international monetary system in jeopardy. The weakness might have been revealed in any event, but the undervaluation of the franc after 1926 sealed the fate of the pound and the international system. The system collapsed in 1931 when Britain, whose balance-of-payments position had been undermined by deflation in the United States, abandoned gold in the wake of the chain reaction initiated by the failure of the big Viennese bank, the Credit Anstalt. All the king's horses could not put the system together again. Some hope for the system was rekindled after United States devaluation in 1934, when the price of gold was raised to $35 an ounce, but by that time the world Depression had become deep, economic nationalism was on the march, and the disease of totalitarianism had spread all over the southern, middle, and eastern parts of the European Continent.

The post-Second World War system built up at Bretton Woods, where the United Nations set up the International Monetary Fund and the World Bank, was an attempt to correct the mistakes of the interwar period by "humanizing" the gold standard. But the IMF was not strong enough in experience, reputation, or resources to replace the authority of the major financial countries, especially, now, the United States. The real power behind the IMF system became the United States, and its instrument was the dollar.

In a technical sense and in fact, the United States became the center of the international monetary system. First, the United States became the sole country pegging its currency to gold; in this sense the dollar became the *key currency*. Second, and partly because of the first event, other countries pegged their currencies to the dollar, either directly or through the pound, franc, or escudo; in this sense the dollar became the primary *intervention currency*. Third, dollars became increasingly used as an international asset for central banks; in this sense the dollar became the primary *reserve currency*. Fourth, the dollar became increasingly used for trading operations as a currency of contract; in this sense the dollar became the primary *vehicle currency* (along with the pound). Fifth, and finally, the dollar was increasingly used as the *currency of quotation;* in this sense the dollar became the main currency used as *unit of account*. In these five roles the dollar became the currency that was more equal than any other just as sterling was in the nineteenth century.

After the war no one doubted the strength of the dollar, and dollars were accumulated by central banks as being more useful than gold because of the interest that could be earned and because the dollar was the currency of intervention in the exchange market. As postwar recovery proceeded, the European countries developed the balance-of-payments surpluses needed to rebuild their reserves. The surpluses were taken out in both dollars and gold as no one doubted the ability of the United States to convert dollars into gold. But in 1958, after the European currencies had become convertible and much stronger, the United States balance-of-payments deficit, which in the early fifties had averaged $1 billion, jumped to $3 billion. Awareness of the implications for convertibility of the dollar became apparent, and central banks took a closer look at their portfolios. Since 1958 the United States has run a deficit of over $2 billion of which, on the average, about half was taken in gold and half in dollars. But many central banks held dollars merely because they did not want to embarrass the United States. Involuntary dollar holdings mounted until France led the way to a "declaration of independence." After the spring of 1965 France began converting its entire surplus into gold, and other countries became increasingly reluctant to expand their holdings of United States dollars. In effect, the world monetary system appeared to be moving back to the gold standard.

Thus we see that since the Second World War the world economy has been moving toward a system which, in some respects, is similar to that of the nineteenth-century gold-standard system, with the dollar, New York, and the Federal Reserve System replacing sterling, London, and the Bank of England. However, the present system is complicated by a Federal Reserve policy that is more ambiguous than the Bank of England used to have. The present system makes use of numerous restrictions and prohibitions, and there is a greater self-consciousness on the part of foreign central banks about the advantages to be gained from a system which relies heavily on the dollar and United States monetary policy.

Let us put these complications aside for a moment, however, and concentrate on some of the institutional features through which the system works. First of all, the United States government forbids its own citizens to hold gold, so that there is no legal gold market in the United States; the center of the world's gold market is London (which, however, is not open to the British public, since the British government also forbids its citizens from holding gold). But the United States is still the main determinant of the market price of gold, since the United States Treasury will sell or buy gold for dollars at $35 an ounce for monetary purposes to foreign central banks, as we saw in Chapter 8. This means, in effect, that the London private-market gold price cannot differ from $35 an ounce by much more than the cost of shipping gold from the United States to London.

Let us see how the gold market works. New gold production, of somewhat more than $1 billion worth a year (the main producer is South Africa, with Russia and Canada of considerably less importance), is marketed through London. Producers sell gold in London. Consumers buy it. Usually the supply exceeds the demand, and the Bank of England takes up the excess gold, paying for it with dollars; it then replenishes its dollar holdings by selling the gold to the United States Treasury or to other central banks. (The Bank of England manages the recently developed "gold pool," by which demand for new gold by other major central banks is managed collectively.) But when the private demand for gold exceeds the supply, the Bank of England sells gold from its own reserve in exchange for dollars and then presents the dollars for conversion to gold at the United States Treasury. Thus United States gold losses or gains are directly dependent on whether there is an excess demand or excess supply of gold in the London market. They also depend on whether other central banks want to keep less or more of their reserves in dollars or gold. United States gold losses over any period of time are thus composed of the excess of private demand for gold over its supply in the private gold market and the excess of dollar holdings of foreign central banks. Russian sales or purchases have to be included in private demands or supplies.

The most important causes of fluctuations in the United States gold stocks, apart from changes in the flow of gold from the mines, are the following:

1. *Russian gold sales.* When the Russians have a poor wheat harvest, they ship gold to London to get dollars to pay for wheat imports, but when their harvest is good, they prefer to add their domestic production of gold to their gold stocks. Thus the United States gold stock goes up when the Russian wheat crop is bad, and down (or up by less) when it is good.

2. *Private hoarding.* When there is an increase or decrease in the speculative demand for gold or in the demand for its use in industry and the arts, the United States gold stock goes correspondingly down or up.

3. *Central bank conversions.* When the other central banks want to alter the composition of their reserves and shift from dollars into gold, the United States suffers a gold loss; and when they want to increase their holdings of dollars at the expense of gold, the United States has a gold gain.

4. *A deficit in the United States balance of payments.* When the United States monetary system creates more money than Americans or private foreign residents want to hold, the flow of dollars offered on foreign-exchange markets abroad expands either directly or indirectly after first raising United States prices or lowering United States interest rates. Since foreign central banks keep their exchange rates fixed to the dollar, they have to buy up the excess dollars on the exchange markets, dollars which they convert into gold at the United

> States Treasury. A lax United States monetary policy therefore induces gold losses, while a restrictive (or not excessively expansive) one induces gold gains.

The first three factors affecting the United States gold stock tend to be rather volatile and suggest that the Federal Reserve System cannot follow as simple or convenient a set of rules for monetary policy as those adopted by the Bank of England in the nineteenth century, tightening monetary policy when there is a gold loss and easing it when there is a gold gain. If the Federal Reserve followed such a rule uncritically, United States monetary policy would be dictated in part by the whims of foreign central banks and private gold hoarders and by Russian wheat harvests. Such a policy on the part of the Federal Reserve System would not be in the interests of the United States or indeed in the interests of the world community as a whole.

This is the justification, in part, for the United States practice of sterilizing gold movements, preventing them, in the first instance, from having an impact on outstanding dollar liabilities. But the process of sterilization is, in fact, probably carried too far. As noted above, gold losses may be due to a deficit in the United States balance of payments arising from excessive credit expansion in the United States. If gold losses arising from excess credit creation in the United States are sterilized, the disequilibrium is perpetuated with no compensating gains. To see this, we can go back to the discussion in Chapter 13, assuming this time a shift of demand from American securities to, say, British securities, the initial impact of which is a gold loss from the United States to Britain.

If the United States authorities did not sterilize the initial gold outflow, gold would eventually come back to the United States in the process of transferring in goods, through a balance-of-payments surplus, the financial transfer implied by the capital movement. It is sometimes argued, however, that unless the authorities sterilize the gold outflow, deflation or unemployment in the United States will result. But there is no reason for deflation or unemployment to result from the transfer process. If no sterilization took place in either the United States or Britain, the British would spend more on all goods, including American goods, while the Americans would spend less on all goods, including British goods. The change in *spending* is not the same as a change in income or employment, and indeed the shift in the international pattern of expenditure could induce inflationary pressure in the United States rather than deflationary pressure.

It is sometimes argued that because the United States is a large country, with only a small proportion of internationally traded goods, the decrease in United States spending on American goods will be large, causing a net fall in spending on American goods and bringing about recession. But the conclusion does not follow because, for precisely the reason the decrease in United States spending on home goods will be high, the increase in foreign spending on United States goods will be high also.

It may next be argued that in all countries, including the United States, many goods are not traded at all, so that there will be a large drop in United States spending on domestic goods and export goods without any corresponding increase in spending by foreigners on United States domestic goods. But because the United States is large, a given change in spending, spread over a wide range of goods, needs to reduce demand only a little in any one sector of the economy, so that price changes also need only be minor. Price changes undoubtedly occur after any disturbance, but international disturbances in a large country with a small international sector are likely to be correspondingly small.

It is partly because of the adoption of this faulty technique of automatic sterilization, based on unsound theory as well as practice, that Britain, the United States, and a few other countries that have followed their bad example have managed to maintain and perpetuate balance-of-payments disequilibriums over a long period of time, to the discomfort of the inhabitants of these countries and at the social cost of the remainder of the world community. The harm is not restricted to a persistent weakness of the pound sterling, and an incipient weakness of the dollar, but extends to the measures adopted in their defense. These measures have included prohibitions on imports, hidden export bounties, altered military-procurement plans, taxes on capital exports, new laws forbidding private gold purchases, and arm-twisting "gentlemen's agreements" with banks. In the case of America these measures have created in the minds of many observers the sorry spectacle of a superpower, a democracy, creating on the basis of a wrong theory and faulty practice, an artificially weak currency, imitating measures invented in Nazi Germany and perpetuated all over Europe in the years following the end of the Second World War. The situation is made more ironic by the fact that America led the battle against those very measures when they were imposed in Europe where to a large extent they have now been abandoned.

Until recently the continental European position has been that the United States should correct its deficit and then make an agreement on international monetary reforms, probably through creating a new reserve asset, while the United States position has been to talk about reform before correcting the deficit. In a formal sense the major countries including the United States have now decided to go ahead with reform, but it is of the kind likely to paper over the cracks in the wallpaper rather than undertake any real replastering.

The case for reform of the system is a strong one, if the rest of the world is unwilling to continue to use the dollar to the extent it formerly did, but it is not clear that the central banks can or will agree on the ingredients constituting an improvement in the world monetary system. Many Europeans have become bitter about the intrusion of American capital into Europe and its buying up European factories—purchases which the Europeans themselves have financed by holding on to dollars needed to lubricate the flow of trade. In another vein they argue that the dollar holdings of the European countries have helped finance the Vietnam war, of which they disapprove. Against this some American economists have insisted that the inadequate capital markets in Europe—inadequate because of Europe's own restrictions—have left European companies no recourse but to use the dollar as a financial intermediary between lenders and borrowers. The dollar is so entrenched, so strong, and so useful that its use will, like the English language, spread over the world—not a very comforting thought to the new nationalism developing on the Continent of Europe. This is how the more extreme views of some European nationalists might be expressed:

The disease of currency
Through the banks hurled
The cancer of the dollar
Buying up the world.

The banks are nervous
About a run on gold
The Americans determine
The price it's sold.

To price it still higher
Making paper gold
Is to make our position
Impossible to hold.

As good as gold
As sound as a buck
At the price it's sold
You need some luck.

Monetary order
Measure of cooperation
We can get along fine
Without your intermediation.

You must restrain
Your vehicle of culture
Language of power
Green portrait of a vulture.

Reparations, amortization
You must begin
Repayment, redemption
Of original sin.

You have borrowed
And we have lent
We have trusted
And gold you've sent.

We have trusted
And you have pledged
The honor of a Republic
Not to be hedged.

What do we want?
We don't want you
We want our factories
Not your rendezvous.

Out, damned buck
From Glasgow to Rome
Give us gold
Yankee, go home.

The dollars you spend
May soon go home
The money you save
May be your own.

This resentment of American financial expansion is not shared by all Europeans, many of whom see great advantages in American capital investments as a medium by which the technology gap between Europe and America can be reduced. But from the standpoint of the world's monetary system, the United States answer to the bitterness is a simple one:

The error in such thinking
Ignores the common ground
That the dollar is a cancer
No cure yet found.

It is in this antagonistic milieu that the managers of the system —the central bankers and the finance ministers—have reached an impasse on the fundamental reform that is necessary. The stability of the system depends entirely on their ability to agree, yet the ingredients for agreement are not present.

The weak link in the present system is the threatened instability in the price of gold, since the United States cannot continue to sell gold and at the same time preserve confidence in the dollar. At present, events are moving on a collision course, which in the absence of cooperation will result in a sporadic and uncontrolled increase in the price of gold. It would be far better to raise the price of gold by agreement than to have this decision forced on the world through the inability of the major powers to cooperate.

Yet it is surely clear that an increase in the price of gold is at best a second best course. The way out, the path of stability, lies in agreement among the main European countries, Japan, and the United States that they need to preserve the present dollar price of gold and will commit their gold reserves to that end. After all, if there can be no agreement on a new system, it is better to make do with the one we now have than to allow the forces of instability to disrupt the unprecedented expansion of industry and trade that has been the outstanding feature of the postwar world economy.

Were the central banks to agree on this, there would have to be a balance of responsibility between the United States, at the center of the system, and the other major countries. A gentlemen's agreement is really necessary while basic reform is being worked out—or at least talked about. Europe and Japan must be willing to alter the composition of their reserves to the extent necessary to preserve the present dollar price of gold. To make Europe's commitment worthwhile, the United States, on its part, would have to be willing and able to preserve the stability of its economy and take international interests into account.*

* One economist, in commenting on this recommendation, which I had made to a congressional committee and to the Board of Governors of the Federal Reserve System in the fall of 1966, complained that I was trying to make "the mice chase the cats" in recommending that Europe and America take each other's interests directly into account in formulating their monetary and gold policies. But as we shall see in the last chapter, "The Cooperative Imperative," there is no alternative to cooperation in a world that is not ready for the cession of national sovereignty to a coercive world monetary authority. Men of passionate interests simply have to direct their attention away from the myopic allure of jealous and narrow national sovereignty toward a more viable ethos based on international cooperation and the rule of law.

III. *Policies*

16. *Inheritance and Progress*

The world is in a state of constant flux. Environment is adapted to wants, and wants alter with circumstances. Ideas, machines, people are born or created, reach fruition, and die, to be replaced by new ideas, new machines, and new generations with different endowments. The flux of life is inexorable, the past can never be reborn, and time is irreversible. You can't go home again.

Let us now play, however, one of the instructive and harmless games of scientists. Let us abstract from the ineluctable logic of the irreversibility of time and banish all unnecessary complications—"mere tricks to show the stretch of human vanity." Let us abstract from the constancy of irreversible change and envisage a *stationary* system.

In a stationary system the life cycle is closed. After completing one cycle, we are back in the position from which we started. People are born, pass through the stages of life, and re-create themselves through their children before they die; machines are constructed, issue their products, depreciate, and are replaced by similar machines; crops are planted, yield their harvest, and are replanted. As the earth orbits the sun, economies and societies oscillate around the fixed point of biological fact—an eternal process chugging away in even rotation in a make-believe world in which each datum is duplicated one earth's rotation (or any other chronometric time unit) hence.

The purpose of this imaginary construction is to help us

glimpse the matching equilibrium of the variables of the economic system. We start with the simplest case: households of all ages in continual activity. Men go out to the fields or factories to work, bring their produce to market at the end of the day, sell their produce to intermediaries (middlemen), and deposit the money proceeds or their salaries at home or in the bank at night; housewives go about their daily chores, take a sum of money from the till, work out a shopping list, deposit money at the stores, and return home with the fruit of their shopping expeditions. Money passes in sequence from the store to the producer, to the shopper, to the store; cash balances fall or rise as emergencies are met or as extra earnings arise. Goods are produced in the field or factories, pass from producers to the store and from the store to the shopper, and are used up at home.

Lifetime plans are made. The cash balance in the till or in the bank rises as receipts of the producer-husband exceed payments of the shopper-wife. Liquidity becomes excessive, and investment plans are made for household durables, for a house, for income at retirement. Excess receipts are taken from the till or the checking account and put into a savings account, yielding interest, while the banker, the credit middleman, lends out the money to the husband-producer, who thus can expand his holdings. The demands for, and supplies of, credit are balanced by interest-rate adjustments.

As the couple matures, income increases, new savings result, and additional outlets for investment are sought. The demand for claims to streams of future receipts of money is satisfied through the markets for stocks and bonds, these streams being supplied by producer-husband firms that need to use the goods the savers have temporarily done without. The demands for, and supplies of, these income streams are equated through price adjustment, the mechanism through which budgetary plans of different households or firms, acting independently, are made compatible on the market.

As the couple ages, they acquire a net worth, provide for the education of their children, and get settled for retirement. Upon retirement they cash in life insurance policies, sell their assets, and consume the stream of income prepared for their postworking life, leaving to their heirs over and above their own cultural heritage whatever remains from their retirement expenditure, their remaining net worth.

The process of generation and regeneration is a miraculous one. Society as a whole is in a state of even rotation, yet individuals get progressively better off as their incomes grow through their working lifetime toward retirement, as throughout life they acquire new skills for producing and maturer tastes for consuming, increasing the possibility of enjoyment, while on the opposite side of the ledger life expectancy inexorably declines, and the human being, in his role as individual, approaches extinction in this world.

How can individuals become perpetually better off (in a sense) while society as a whole preserves a constancy of aggregate income? The mystery is dispelled if we look at the components of the human population as biological organisms. Every year couples are retiring and being replaced in their positions by those a year younger, who in turn are replaced by those a year younger than themselves, and so on down to those just entering productive life; analogous people are passing out of our make-believe world and coming into it. The life cycle is one of perpetual motion and perpetual betterment, but the social organism—society as a whole—stands still.

The circular flow of money also contains a miracle: demand for, and supply of, all things taken as a whole, including money, are always in balance. Let us see how this comes about. Husband-producers are continually receiving money from their selling or borrowing, while housewife-consumers are continually paying money for their purchases of goods, services, and securities. But each unit pays for any gap between receipts and payments by reducing or increasing hoards. This is true of the household couple; it is true of firms; it is true of banks, and other intermediaries; it is true of governments. If, on balance, some decision units are running down their cash balances, other units must be building up their cash balances by an equal amount. Thus any excess of all receipts over all spending by any single unit has its counterpart in an excess supply of goods, exactly equal to the excess demand for money. For all units in the system there can be no excess demand for, or supply of, all things.

The circular flow of receipts and payments, the balancing of budgets through liquidity constraints, the continual balancing of demands and supplies through price adjustments, and the life cycle of regeneration—involving millions of goods, entities, and instruments of production—reach a marvelous equilibrium in which the budget plans of the different units are made compatible with one another through the medium of the market. Every activity of every entity in the system has a bearing on every other entity, remote as the connection may be. Nothing escapes the mutual interdependence of general equilibrium.

But having seen the marvel of this evenly rotating system, let us give it up to reintroduce those things abstracted from. Let us shift from our make-believe system to the real world. The key factor rendering the concept of an even rotation unrealistic is *bequest*.

Bequest implies a change in circumstances from one generation to the next. A constant bequest is consistent with the evenly rotating system in equilibrium, but an increasing or decreasing bequest is incompatible with it. Yet the concept of a constant bequest is implausible for the human species, if it is not absolutely impossible.

The reason lies in the nature of knowledge, the transmission of culture through language, and the process of evolutionary selection. A generation accumulates and consumes commodities and can easily ensure a constant bequest of goods from one generation to the next. But allow a single new idea to be communicated through the system and to remain in it, and two cycles can never be the same. It is largely because of the possibility of bequest, the most important of bequests being knowledge, that societies do not merely repeat themselves, but progress. In knowledge lies a key to social progress.

A couple produce and rear children, grow old, and disappear from the system. But communication is fungible, and the experiences of the older generation can allow the younger generation to begin productive life with whatever it can salvage of the mistakes and successes of the past. Inventions get circulated throughout the economy and affect productivity. Old machines are replaced by better ones. Recorded history itself provides a source of accumulated knowledge biasing society as a whole in the direction of change. Knowledge can be destroyed (forgotten) as well as accumulated if the intergenerational culture-carrying mechanisms break down, of course, and change is not always in the direction of progress toward the betterment of mankind.

Another great form (or determiner) of bequest governing progress lies in natural selection. Those biological characteristics of the population that are best adapted and able to cope with the challenge of society have greater chances of survival, while society itself is molded out of the population it influences. Institutions too meet the challenge or succumb to it. Efficient firms survive; inefficient ones drop out as competition presses them out of existence.

Millions of years ago Homo sapiens—wise man—got hold of something, by chance or fortune, no other species had. We might say that Homo sapiens had a comparative advantage in developing, as a species, the use of intelligence. Take a look at the silly beast. Poor defenseless man, lacking great strength or natural physical defenses, had to rely on his pitiful wit. Only the best could survive, but the best got better as natural selection gave wit survival value. Wit was the only hope for man, with his curious and otherwise inadequate physical equipment.

Pitiful as a mere brain must have seemed millions of years ago, it was the best thing man had, and had man been physically efficient or strong like an elephant, he would not have had to rely on his brain. But his brain had great potential. With it man could exploit, not merely the tediously slow biological evolutionary process, but something entirely new—*social accumulation.* By luck or chance again, the great breakthrough occurred when man learned to pass knowledge from one generation to another and accumulate it. Other species could pass knowledge, but man could store it. Sometime a few thousand years ago he learned to communicate and store communication, freeing man from the restraints of a slow biological evolution to the breakneck speed of social evolution, one generation being able, from the standpoint of knowledge, to stand on the shoulders of the previous generation.

It was this advantage that gave man the chance to conquer, and perhaps destroy, his planet.

17. *Cooperation and Metatrade*

Man's comparative advantage as a species lay, as we have seen, in the use of the brain, his (relatively) strongest resource, and this led him, by accident or design, to the social organism the brain gave him the capacity to develop. Social organization presupposed cooperation. Cooperation is a form of trade, involving transactions, and the rules of efficient cooperation imply specialization along the lines of comparative advantage. But we have to see whether the gains from conventional trade in goods are the same as, or differ in degree or kind from, the gains from trade in the form of cooperative action.

The gains from conventional trade along the lines of comparative advantage can be substantial because such trade permits a division of labor and specialization in activities where all individuals, provinces, and nations produce those goods for which their resources best suit them. Over time their resources change, and this alters the direction profitable specialization takes. Thus in the early years of the nineteenth century America, Germany, and Russia were all exporters of raw materials and grain, while Britain, the industrial leader of the world, specialized in manufactures, mainly textiles, and machinery. But as capitalism progressed in America and Germany, and later Russia, these countries became increasingly competitive in manufacturing and became exporters of products that required a high proportion of capital relative to labor for their manufacture.

Because comparative advantage is a dynamic concept, although for illustrative purposes static (timeless) examples are sometimes used, government policies have to take into account the possibilities for the future development of industry and agriculture. Most countries impose tariffs on goods from other countries either to protect existing industries from foreign competition or to encourage the development of new industries. These tariffs create waste, from the standpoint of the world economy, because they encourage industries to develop in parts of the world where specialization in other products is more efficient. But from the national point of view, one country in isolation expects to gain from the industrial development it expects tariff protection to stimulate.

There is no world authority to impose the requirement of freer trade on each country, and as long as this authority does not exist, countries will persist in acting in national, rather than international, interest. It is surely true that if the United States government (or more exactly the United States Constitution) permitted the states to impose tariffs on one another's products, they would end up doing so against the national interest, and trade between the individual states of America would become as restricted as trade is among the nations of the world. Much of the secret of United States wealth lies in the fact that the inhabitants and firms of each state in the Union have been able to specialize along the lines of comparative advantage, without interstate barriers.

Many of the less developed countries have tried to develop modern industries. To stimulate their development, the governments of these countries have protected particular products by tariffs or import restrictions. A tariff implies a subsidy on the domestic production of the product and a tax on its consumption so that, as governments that are aware of the implications of their own policy realize, the effect of an import tariff on a good is to discourage its domestic consumption and to encourage its domestic production. For example, India in effect protects steel products and fertilizer; Argentina, Brazil, Columbia, and Peru put heavy tariffs on automobiles; and the Common Market countries provide heavy protection to agriculture.

The long-run rationale of this protective policy, which interferes with efficiency in the short run and imposes a cost on the countries involved, is the belief that the countries can develop comparative advantages along these lines in the future. It is questionable whether the use of resources to produce automobiles represents an efficient allocation of Peru's or Columbia's scarce resources, whether Indian heavy industry is the best place to invest scarce foreign exchange when India's agriculture and fertilizer industries are undeveloped, and whether the Common Market countries can develop an efficient producer of agricultural products. But the experts in these countries think so—or, if not, that there are political gains to the policy that are high enough to offset the economic losses.

In the long run, exports must pay for imports. In the short run, cash reserves or foreign-exchange balances can be used up, and temporary resort to borrowing is possible; but in the long run, any decision to reduce imports involves a corresponding decision to reduce exports. Thus any county that decides to embark on a policy of *import substitution* (substitution of home production for imports), a policy that has achieved great popularity in the less developed countries, at the same time decides to embark on a policy of *export inhibition.* A tariff on imports has a stifling effect on imports in the short run and an equally stifling effect on exports in the long run. Policies of import substitution are, in fact, the basic cause of the stagnation of the exports of less developed countries like Turkey, India, and Argentina over the past fifteen years.

The gains from trade can be reduced, as I have indicated, by tariffs. That is indeed why there is constant tariff-negotiation activity in Geneva, where the members of the General Agreement on Tariffs and Trade (GATT) meet to bargain over tariff reductions.

The gains from tariff negotiation can be substantial, but there is an even greater opening for gains from trade than through reduction in the tariffs of ordinary goods. For I have really been speaking, up to now, of trade in ordinary goods, and have not mentioned metatrade—trade in what can be called *magical goods.* (They are sometimes referred to as *public goods* or *environmental goods.*) Ordinary goods cost real resources to produce and distribute, so that the more one gives up of a good, the less one has of it. Magical goods are goods that, while they may cost resources to produce, remain in existence and can be consumed by anybody at all.

Bread is an ordinary good because its enjoyment is divided between people; the more one gets of it, the less somebody else gets of it. But an idea is a magical good because its consumption by one person need not detract from its consumption by any other person. Shoes, buttons, and wine are ordinary goods, but discoveries, television programs, defense, and, to some extent, education are magical goods.

The gains from trade in ordinary goods can be extensive, as I argued before. But the gains from trade in magical goods can be phenomenal. The reason is clear. For trade in ordinary goods there is a cost to exporting, and the only reason one accepts the cost is that he values the imports he gets more than the exports he gives up. But for trade in magical goods there is no cost to exporting (there is often even a gain), and still one receives something in return. I shall call trade in magical goods *metatrade.*

It is easy to see how large is the class of activities that come under the heading of metatrade. If an entrepreneur gets enjoyment from his role as an organizer of the factors of production and still gets paid handsomely for it, he is profiting from metatrade. If a scientist or artist is inwardly compelled to creative activity and still finds that society is willing to compensate him for it, he is engaging in metatrade. If a workman enjoys his work, an artisan takes pride in his craftsmanship, a teacher finds fulfillment in conveying the art of discovery—in all these cases there is a double payment, the pleasure of working, or "exporting," and the pecuniary reward from it. Indeed, one of the objects of modern social organization is to widen the class of metatransactions. As D. H. Lawrence put it,

> *Work, if it's never any fun*
> *If it doesn't absorb you*
> *Like an absorbing game,*
> *Don't do it.*

The gains from metatrade in the field of international economics and politics are so considerable that they deserve explicit mention. Consider two countries that have imposed tariffs on imports from each other. Each decides that its own tariffs are harmful to itself and to the other. They meet and make concessions to one another in the form of tariff reductions. This is *metatrade*, that is, trade in magical goods, insofar as each country acting alone would benefit from its own tariff reduction; it may be giving up something (in exchange for a gift from the other country) it wants to give up anyway. Thus there is a double gain, that from the reduction in one's own tariff and that from the reduction in the other country's tariff.

As an even stronger example, consider military expenditures in two countries formerly antagonistic to one another. Suppose disarmament negotiations begin, and concessions are made in the form of reductions in military expenditure. Each country gains from the reduction in the former opponent's expenditure because that reduction reduces the threat to its security. But it also gains from the reduction in its own expenditure, since the resources can now be used for production of consumption goods. This is another clear case of metatrade, and one can find similar examples in the ending of wars, in treaties, in conventions (for example, the convention that people drive cars on an established side of the street), in the sharing of artistic accomplishments, culture, and scientific research, and in mutual protection against diseases.

18. *Complex Choice and Government*

Cooperation involves joint decision making. This usually implies organizational forms such as government in which the process is formalized and institutionalized. The theory of complex decision making is an extension of choice theory. We considered choice theory in some detail in Chapter 3; now we need to explore its ramifications in institutions where conflicts arise and where decisions are made difficult by competing interests or conflicting objectivity.

In scientific analysis and in history it has often been found useful to utilize one's own experiences with optimizing behavior by extending them to more complex groups such as families, nations, or unions, starting off with the hypothesis that each group has a clear interest to maximize. Thus historians often speak of the national traits or characteristics of a people as if a nation were a single entity possessing a common spirit, a unified purpose, an *élan vital,* and so forth. We stereotype the Frenchman, the Englishman, the German, and the Italian with the distilled essence of the national characteristics that most impress us, while recognizing the diversity of the actual inhabitants that make up the stereotype. When we generalize, our thought processes simplify the complexity of actual reality into stereotype notions that are in one sense always wrong and yet contain a kernel of vital truth. The communication of information contains inaccuracies and oversimplifications that are unavoidable whenever we try to make complex reality simple enough to articulate.

Let us now, however, try an alternative course. We can reverse the direction of the analogy and apply the complexity of the corporate state or the diverse groups within it to simpler entities like the individual. That is to say, while one possibility is to apply the theory of the individual to the theory of government in order to recognize what it is that gives government its *unifying* characteristics, we can also apply the theory of government to an individual in order to recognize man in his *diverse* features—to recognize man for what he really is, a complex being coordinated by the need to weld together into a single acting organism the different stresses and strains of his personality. We can see this best if we start off with the most primitive of all human beings, the infant.

An infant contains the seeds of government but not the actuality. He is helpless precisely because he cannot integrate the elementary choice cells he contains. He contains multitudes of choice cells and cannot bring them together under a single government.

As he grows and learns, he develops control over particular dimensions of biological and social activity. At first he can only perceive ordinal variations—register "more" or "less" on his utility scale—but as he grows, he learns to discriminate between different sources of enjoyment (goods) and to recognize their different want-satisfying powers. Starting from the elementary knowledge that he wants more milk rather than less, he develops in a great jump into the awful reality of a world of complex choice by way of the realization that he prefers another spoonful of pablum to another suck of milk, and a good burp to either. The first government is thus formed with its power to integrate, in more or less successful degree, the complex tastes of hunger, thirst, and gastronomical freedom.

But our young person is not yet a mature person, and will not be until more governments form and are integrated in a hier-

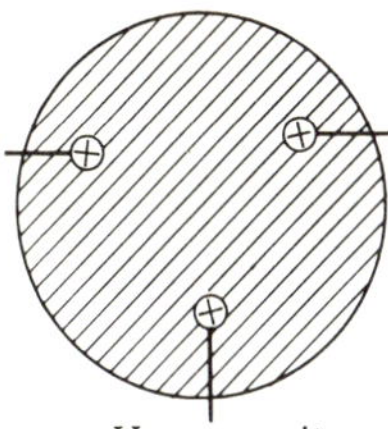

archical chain of command as complex as that of a modern army. He learns to prefer some people to others, say, mother to grandmother, grandmother to father, and therefore—if he is consistent, and becoming consistent is itself a big jump—mother to father. Two dimensions of taste, food and other people, are now formed, with more to come, and the terrible reality of a new choice becomes necessary. Given his opportunity set, our young person forms a senior government to integrate his choice process on a centralized level. Different dimensions are brought

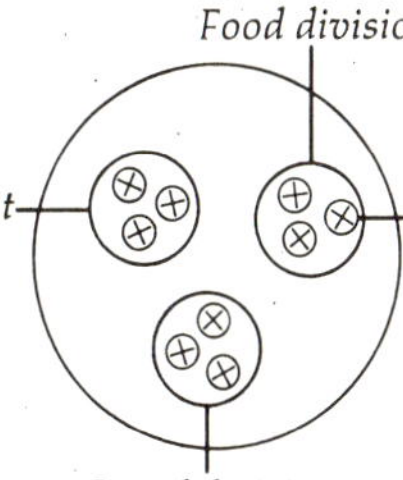

under the dictatorship of this new higher government, although efforts of the party chiefs of each decentralized unit to escape the tyranny of the central government are ever present, and unless the new government is strongly rooted in natural self-interest (instinct) or possesses adequate coercive power, its power grab will fail until stronger centripetal forces emerge.

The act of forming a higher government is a difficult process even for two dimensions of activity within the child himself. Self-interest requires that each dimension of choice will gain from union, and the stages are diplomatic approach, foreign relations, and finally the cession of sovereignty of each individual choice unit. The ingredients of mutual self-interest make union profitable and make union with one entity preferable to union with another. Thus the government in charge of the taste for lemon drops finds an affinity with the government in charge of the taste for Tootsie Rolls, the *spillover*, or *neighborhood effects* (the effects of one entity's action on other entities) being especially strong. Each then gives up some aspect of its sovereignty to a czar of candy who integrates the sweet-tooth decisions. But mutual self-interest soon recognizes the conflicts and complementaries implicit in choices of candy, meat, and other foods, and new and higher governments are formed, either on an association basis or according to the rules of dictatorship.

And so the child matures. One integration after another, new governments at higher and higher levels encompassing myriads of junior governments in a hierarchical form under the suzerainty of the central government of an increasingly complete being.

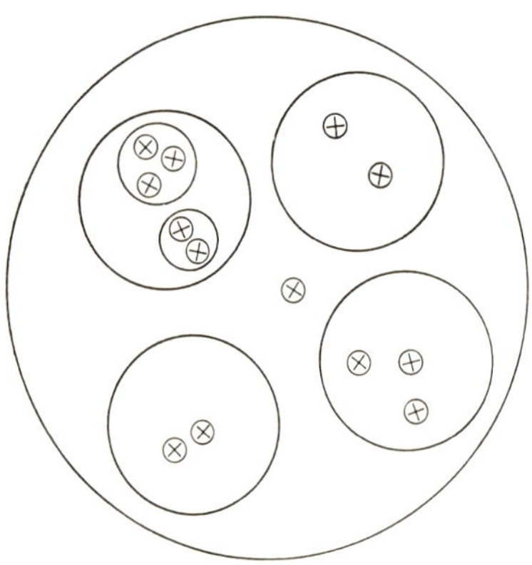

Family units join in. The mother and child begin as interconnected entities. At conception the mother is absolute dictator, but growth in the womb signals the beginnings of a lifelong struggle for independence and liberty. As independent decision cells develop before and after birth, the sphere of individual decisions widens, and the control-dominance of the mother weakens. Physical dominance is gradually replaced by social dominance, and human society becomes more complex. Interrelated control systems develop, with each individual in the family ceding part of his sovereignty to the collective government, whether that be dominated by the father or mother or by a democratically organized decision process.

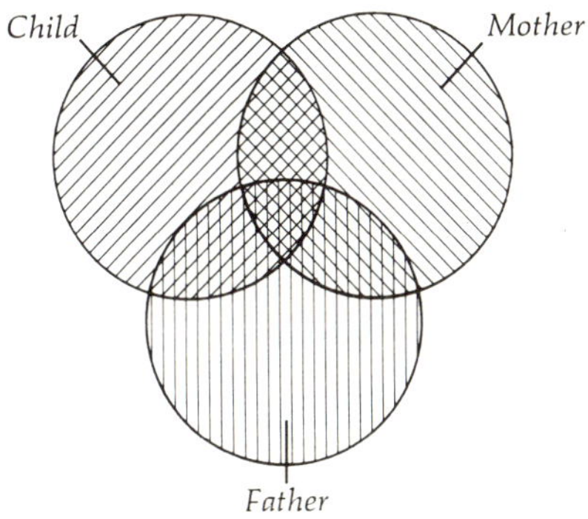

More complex social interrelations grow. All entities develop foreign relations with the outside world—independent of the family and of their roles as part of the family. Spillover effects again indicate the need for more complex governments, the shaded area in the diagram being the area of connections overlapping with the outside world.

Interests are formed with friends, neighbors, and the community. Community organizations develop, foreign relations connect a community with other communities, and intercommunity bodies are formed to supervise choices within the

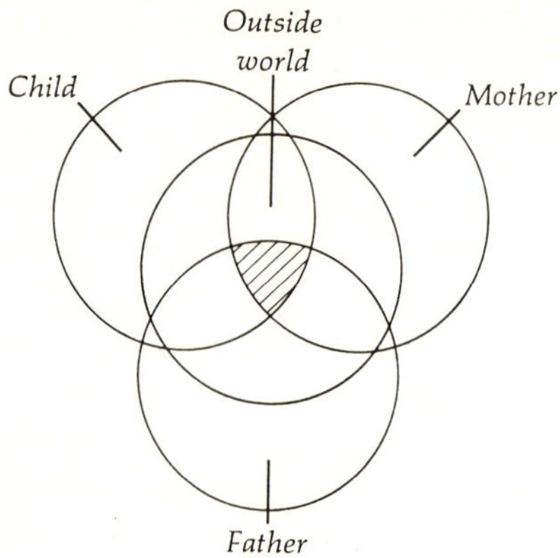

sphere of mutual interest. Local governments establish wider connections, find they have overlapping interests, and find it advisable to formalize these in a hierarchical command chain; senior governments are formed at a greater level of centralization. National choice units develop on the basis of authority delegated from independent family choice units or authority delegated from community or state organizations. And finally mutual interests and antagonisms create the need for a partial delegation of authority to a forum where world interests are taken into account.

The mutual interdependence of human activities thus gives rise to the need for social interest groups and for governments. This raises the problem of the precise nature of the decision-making process and the way this process is related to the system of control in society.

Let us illustrate the problem of complex multidimensional decision making by considering a family about to decide which of three cities it is going to live in. Let us suppose the cities are San Francisco, London, and New York. The decision, it is assumed, is based on three dimensions: the quality of the firm at which the head of the household will work; the standard of living each job offers; and the environment, encompassing the beauty of each city, the spirit of its people, and other intangible factors.

The process of decision making will be very complicated in reality, but let us simplify it a little by supposing a democratically organized three-unit family. Let us suppose the father pays special attention to the quality of the firm, the mother pays special attention to the standard of living, and the children pay special attention to environment. All three places are in some sense acceptable to everyone, but all want to make the best decision possible, so they rank each prospect according to whether it is excellent, good, or only fair.

After some thought (and perhaps considerable research), they come out with the following choices: The father, paying special attention to the quality of the firm, says that New York is excellent, London is good, and San Francisco is fair. The mother, paying special attention to the standard of living, says that San Francisco is excellent, New York is good, and London is fair. The children, paying special attention to environment, says that London is excellent, San Francisco is good, and New York is fair.

The rankings of each city, then, are as follows:

	New York	*London*	*San Francisco*
Father	1	2	3
Mother	2	3	1
Children	3	1	2

Thus the father ranks New York over London and London over San Francisco, the mother ranks San Francisco over New York and New York over London, and the children rank London over San Francisco and San Francisco over New York.

It has turned out that the tastes of the three units of the family society are not homogeneous, so that no unambiguous rankings among the cities emerge. All interests cannot be served, so the society, being democratic, decides to vote on the question, two cities at a time.

The first vote is on New York compared to London. Only the children vote for London over New York, so, by the principle of majority rule, New York wins over London. The second vote is on London compared to San Francisco. The mother votes for San Francisco, but the father and children vote for London. Hence London wins over San Francisco. Thus the family votes for New York over London and for London over San Francisco. This would seem to mean that New York is preferred over San Francisco. After all, if New York is better than London and London is better than San Francisco, New York should certainly, a fortiori, be better than San Francisco.

But a surprise is in store. Just for the fun of it, the family votes between New York and San Francisco. To the astonishment of all, they find that while the father votes for New York over San Francisco, the mother and children vote for San Francisco over New York. San Francisco wins over New York.

But this is impossible. The household prefers New York over London, London over San Francisco, and San Francisco over New York according to the system of decision making its members agreed upon! Their preferences as a group are cyclically inconsistent, and they cannot make a decision by majority voting. They have come up against the so-called Arrow's paradox, named after K. J. Arrow, who, in his book *Social Choice and Individual Values,* analyzed the importance of this situation in democratic political structures.

Of course if we had made things easy by saying that each family unit preferred, say, New York to London and London to San Francisco, then the family would as a group prefer New

York to San Francisco, and its decision would have been clear-cut. But it cannot be doubted that groups are often confronted with almost irreconcilable conflicts of the type mentioned and that this is a central difficulty running through group choice.

This difficulty affects decisions related to the theory of policy that we considered earlier. Suppose that the economic advisers to the President are worried about an incipient recession, a gold outflow, and the need to expand trade with other nations; and suppose, bearing in mind that the advisers know they need three instruments to affect the three targets, that they ask the Federal Reserve Board, the Treasury Department, and the Commerce Department to rank tight money, lower taxes, and lower tariffs in the appropriate order, with each agency paying special attention to a particular sphere. The Federal Reserve Board is to rank the policies with respect to their effects on the balance of payments, Treasury with respect to the recession, and Commerce with respect to their effect on trade. After due deliberation the agencies rank their preferences as follows:

	Instruments		
Target	*Federal Reserve (balance of payments)*	*Treasury (recession)*	*Commerce (trade)*
Tight money	1	3	2
Lower taxes	2	1	3
Lower tariffs	3	2	1

If they now vote democratically, it turns out that tight money is preferred to lower taxes, lower taxes are preferred to lower tariffs, and lower tariffs are preferred to tight money! Again a group contradicts itself.

It would be easy to find dozens of other examples in international politics, with its tough choices—and indeed in every field in which group choice is relevant. But as you might suspect, group conflict merely reveals contradictions that are inherent in most individuals. For the individual is a miniature society.

Suppose I am contemplating the choice of a mate and have three girl friends. Let us call them X, Y, and Z and suppose they are all equally wealthy. Suppose I rank them in terms of the three qualities, apart from wealth, I consider important as follows:

	Qualities		
Girl	*Beauty*	*Character*	*Intellect*
X	*1*	*3*	*2*
Y	*2*	*1*	*3*
Z	*3*	*2*	*1*

Thus X is best on grounds of beauty, followed by Y and then by Z; Y is best on grounds of character, followed by Z and then by X; and Z is best on grounds of intellect, followed by X and then by Y. How can I choose among them?

If I attached equal importance to beauty, character, and intellect and compared the girls on a two-by-two basis from choice, I would find that X > Y, Y > Z, and Z > X—the kind of contradiction we have already noted. How is it possible that I can contradict myself thus? Or rather, is it possible?

One answer was provided by Walt Whitman: "So I contradict myself? Very well then, I contradict myself. I am large, and I contain multitudes."*

We do indeed contain multitudes. In my role as an appraiser of three women on grounds of beauty I do not contradict myself; that is a single dimension of choice. The same is true with respect to intellect and character. But when I come to reconciling

* Quoted in Peter Newman, *The Theory of Exchange*, 1965, p. 176n.

different dimensions—incomparables—I seem in conflict with myself. I find it difficult to trade off the incomparables of intellect, character, and beauty.*

Now if I had perfect freedom, I might see if I could not satisfy the contradiction by taking all three girls and enjoying X for her beauty, Y for her character, and Z for her intellect. But alas, that would probably not be possible.

So I am forced to choose despite my contradictions. To make the decision, I have to coerce my contradictory parts by weighing the importance of the pulls this way and that. We can call this discipline or self-discipline, but as should be clear by now, it is really *government*—government applied to the individual. We generally speak of government in relation to multiple entities, but if we are to think of ourselves as each composed of a multitude of elementary choice cells, we have every right to speak of governing those dimensions in a single general will.

The first task of my government is to maintain order, to resolve the anarchy of contradiction, and to enforce decision where decision is needed. In making the choice, it will have to look more carefully at both the voting procedure and the weights to be assigned to different dimensions of choice.

Let us suppose first that the voting procedure is altered so that we count third choices. If we look at the Table of the Three Girls on page 176, we see that each one of the girls has a first, second, and third place, so that everything is perfectly symmetrical. There is no reason for preferring one to the other until we rank the qualities beauty, character, and intellect in some order. But there is no contradiction except that implied by a very specific two-by-two voting procedure.

To make a decision, I have to rank attributes according to some

* The importance of the concept of incomparability is emphasized in an unpublished paper by V. C. Walsh and H. Putnam, although I should not want to commit them to the present example of it.

scale. If I attach more importance to beauty than to intellect and more importance to intellect than to character, do I then have the ingredients of consistent choice?

If I now vote, I will find that $X > Y$ on beauty and intellect, $Y > Z$ on beauty and character, and $Z > X$ on character and intellect. We can perhaps discount the fact that Y is preferred to X on character, since that is ranked lowest, but we have more trouble in discounting Z's edge over X in both character and intellect. The problem is still there, although there is a sense in which X has gone to the head of the list. But to make things conclusive, it would be necessary to assign numerical values to the elements of the table.

We need not pursue this example further. The important fact is that government as defined here is needed to ensure decisions in the face of competing objectives for the individual, the family, and all compound social choice units.

Government is easy when the governed have similar preferences. If the girls could all be ranked in the same order according to beauty, intellect, and character, the decision process would have been easy. If San Francisco, London, and New York could all be ranked by job, salary, and environment in a unique order, the family decision would have been easy. If tight money, lower taxes, and reduced tariffs all contributed to the gold stock, employment, and trade, the policy decision would have been easy. Similarly, a nation is in harmony with its own government when the interests of the electorate are homogeneous, or at least when the electorate has preferences relatively similar to those of the representatives it elects. Democratic government is easier when mass psychology rules, when people hold the same opinions at the same time.

The problems become difficult when the governed have divergent preferences; this poses innumerable problems and requires either compromise or the exercise of authority.

People are persuaded to do things by reason of self-interest, duty, love, or coercion. Government always involves an element of coercion. The individual's personal government may impose, by way of its preference order, a single taste on the rest. In the case of the family, one member may dictate. And in many governments the interests of a particular race or class may dominate. This is a case of dictatorship and has its counterpart, in the theory of individual preferences, in what has been called lexicographic behavior. This is akin to an animal's instinct, in which rules and priorities dominate. Lexicographic preferences are preferences that rank objects of choice as letters in a dictionary, priority being given first to one attribute, with secondary considerations becoming relevant only in the case of ties. Without such a system of priorities—which is itself an element of dictatorship—complex decision making would be virtually impossible.

19. *Spillover Effects and Manners*

Two centuries ago, in the *The Wealth of Nations,* Adam Smith developed and popularized a compellingly attractive doctrine of nonintervention known as *laissez aller* and *laissez faire;* literally, the terms mean "let pass" and "let make." Let people and goods pass freely through the different parts of the nation and globe, and let businessmen manufacture what they want, for by acting in their selfish interest they will, unconsciously, in general, be advancing the general interest.

> The individual . . . neither intends to promote the public interest, nor knows how much he is promoting it. . . . He intends only his own security . . . his own gain . . . and he is in this led by an invisible hand to promote an end which was no part of his intention. . . . Pursuing his own interest he frequently promotes that of the society more effectually than when he really intends to promote it. . . .

This doctrine was intended as a general guide to policy in an age when bureaucratic laws, controls, and regulations had inhibited the expansion of trade and manufacturing. Mercantilism was in the saddle, and economic thought was dominated by the idea that exports were good, imports were bad, and a nation's wealth consisted of its gold hoard. Against these naïve conceptions Smith put forth the proposition that the purpose of exporting was to be able to import, and that a nation's real wealth consisted of its accumulated stock of goods, not its hoard of the precious metals.

Out of Smith's ideas grew a new orthodoxy, one stressing the virtues of free trade and free competition. Smith's concept of competition and free trade culminated, in its impact on policy, in the free-trade movement in Britain in the middle of the nineteenth century; in the literature of economics it led to the theorem that, barring certain exceptions, free competition and free trade would promote a maximum social welfare, at least in the sense that waste would be eliminated. If individual utilities depend only on the goods individuals themselves consume, if there are no artificial monopolies or collusive actions on the part of groups, if production takes place under conditions in which the instruments of production receive their marginal products, and if, finally, there are no neighborhood effects in production or consumption activities, then it can be proved mathematically that the free play of private initiative will lead to an efficient social solution. Efficiency here must be thought of as a position in which no individuals can be made better off without other persons being made worse off. In other words, the system is one in which there is no waste.

These assumptions are not, of course, met in reality, but neither is the concept of social welfare implied very relevant. For any given state of economic organization the existence of spillover (neighborhood) effects, or *externalities*, would mean that society would not achieve, in the absence of government intervention, a maximum product or a social optimum. (This does not mean that government intervention will lead to a social optimum; utopias are not for this world.) Those industries that yielded external diseconomies, that is, those industries producing harmful by-products causing damage or creating costs for others, would tend to produce too much for the good of society. An example would be a factory that belched smoke from its chimneys, creating a spillover effect that would reduce the enjoyment of other people. On the other hand, those industries that yielded external economies (created benefits for others) would tend to underproduce. For these reasons there is an argument for interfering with free competition by taxing industries that produce harmful side effects and subsidizing industries that produce beneficial side effects.

The argument can, however, be carried much too far. Externalities have a useful role to play, and it is often beneficial in the long run for society to do nothing about them. Their useful role derives from the stimulus they provide to the reorganization of social groups. Thus a beneficial side effect emanating from industry X that can be captured by industry Y may simply mean that firms in industry X and firms in industry Y should merge and produce their outputs jointly. Supermarkets and shopping centers are really little more than the outcome of a rational process of exploiting what were once externalities (shoppers pay a fixed transportation cost to get to a store or shopping center and hence there is a gain to centralization of shopping activities) through a process of internalizing them in joint activity.

Examples of unexploited externalities can be seen all over the world. In European countries, as well as in the less developed countries of the Southern Hemisphere, great unexploited externalities exist in the fields of social and business organization, as can be seen by even the most casual glance at the decentralized shopping facilities and the inadequately financed organizations of higher learning. Some of these unexploited opportunities provide openings for huge profits for enterprising investors and do not require government intervention. The purpose of externalities of many types is to act as a guide to the formation of privately profitable social and business groups. Government is itself, of course, an institution of society, and it has its own sphere of legitimate activity. Private pressure groups cannot easily form, or at least have not formed, to provide self-policing of pollution problems.

Of course the externalities associated with pollution problems will alter the nature of society if they are left alone. Firms that produce smoke nuisances as a by-product will get "punished" in the long run as the cities they are in become less comfortable places to inhabit; this change will eventually make these firms unprofitable. But the fact that this long "punishment" process is under way may be cold comfort to the city residents. For in the meantime, life in the great cities can be reduced to a shell of former activity, and all the inhabitants can be made to suffer a cost out of all proportion to the penalty slowly being inflicted on the firm. Why should the residents of the Los Angeles area be driven from their cities because of the smoke and dirt gushing from industrial chimneys? Why should the 3 billion inhabitants of the world have to pay the price of a polluted atmosphere for the sake of the expense saved to particular industries in constructing converters and other means of protecting their neighbors from the smoke nuisance they create?

Even if punishment is deliberately imposed by the community through the market or directly, the community may have to bear a cost far in excess of the penalty delivered to the socially obnoxious firms. One reason for this disproportionate cost is that the time it takes to inflict the penalty is far longer than the time horizons with which individuals are ordinarily concerned. It may take several years before irresponsible firms are found out, whereas the harm they inflict may have immediate and permanent consequences even though those consequences are not immediately perceived by the public or the government.

But let us suppose that nothing is done to mitigate the health hazard caused by smoke nuisance. Communities would be driven from those areas of greatest concentration to those areas, perhaps toward the mountains, where residual areas of clean air remained. Rents would rise in places with clean air and fall in cities where the pollution hazard was greatest.

New opportunities for profitable investment would arise. Clean air commands a premium over dirty air, and a price would be paid for it. Facilities would develop for manufacturing pure air, and a market for air would be developed just as a market for water developed in Europe after the residents of many big cities of the Continent allowed their sewage systems to spoil their water. Whether sold by the bottle or by the deep breath, clean air would cease to be a free good.

Homes and factories would be built with air-purifying ventilation systems, and activities would cease to be conducted outdoors. Increasing waves of smog would blacken windows and make them obsolete, and artificial light would be substituted for sunlight. Life would increasingly be conducted indoors and underground. The structure of cities would change. Open streets would be replaced by covered streets, and facilities would be created for expelling dirty air into the atmosphere now rendered useless for human use. Forays into the hazardous realm of the atmosphere would become infrequent and possibly would be made only with gas masks like those used by British and German soldiers on the battlefield of Ypres and currently needed in Japanese playgrounds adjacent to the big factories.

Character would alter over time, since a new Darwinian selection process would support those capable of thriving in crowded underground living quarters at the expense of the "retarded"—those fitted only for open spaces, sunshine, and clean air. The mole would be driven by the technically superior human being above ground to take over a new environment now perhaps prepared to his liking, and Hades would be our new paradise. Am I exaggerating? Let us hope so. But it should not be thought that externalities like smoke hazards are exceptional.

Externalities are, technically, those benefits or costs of decisions not accruing to the choice unit in question, but rather received or paid by others. They run throughout society, but certain of them are so generally accepted by custom that they are not readily identifiable.

Suppose you are sitting somewhere on a beach and a person sits nearby and starts to play a radio. This affects your enjoyment of the beach (increasing or decreasing it), and you may decide to stay and listen or move away. Suppose you stay. But now the person makes it louder and louder. You may still enjoy the program, but you will probably edge away until it suits the pitch of your ear. By playing the radio louder, your neighbor on the beach invades your own social territory, forcing you to defend it (by getting him to stop) or flee.

Next suppose he opens a lunch bag and starts eating loudly and scatters the containers around you. This is a second intrusion, a new invasion. And then he is joined by friends who all loudly talk inanities you cannot help hearing. You may still stay, but if all this goes on, you will eventually reach what William James called a pain threshold—a point at which you will have to react.

The toothpaste and mouthwash companies exploit intuitive knowledge of spillover effects in their advertising campaigns. House owners who pitch their garbage in the street create spillover effects. Conversationalists create spillover effects in producing pleasure or displeasure in other people, quite apart from the pleasure they themselves derive from conversation. Spillover effects may be positive for some and negative for others.

The production of a painting may create spillover effects out of all proportion to the gain to the painter. The world can still enjoy the paintings of Leonardo and Goya and Van Gogh quite apart from the personal rewards these artists received in their lifetime.

A community may educate its young exceptionally well but lose them to another community when they grow up—a negative spillover effect (a *spillout*) from their point of view, a positive one (a *spillin*) from the other community's point of view. On the other hand the first community may hire people from other communities at a gain over and above cost, a gain due to the training they received elsewhere.

An individual may play a role in his community that grants a subsidy of his time to the community out of all proportion to the rewards that he in his self-interest, narrowly interpreted, would accept.

These are but a few examples of externalities. Some are good; some should and can be corrected; some are intractable or too costly to overcome.

One means of moving toward greater efficiency is to tax negative spillouts and subsidize spillins. Those factories belching smoke can be taxed to compensate the human beings affected. Suppose a fraction of the smoke, say 20 percent, disappears from the atmosphere and does not harm anyone. Of the 80 percent remaining, suppose 40 percent of the total smoke is localized, affecting directly the city population, while another 20 percent is distributed over the state, 15 percent over the nation, and the rest (5 percent) over the world as a whole. Then 50 percent of the tax should be returned to the city government, 25 percent to the state government, 18.75 percent to the Federal government, and the rest to a world government —if it existed.

When spillover effects involve calculable gains, such as those involved in the production of knowledge through research or the production of beauty through artistic endeavor, the beneficiaries of the gains can be taxed to pay the creators. But it is not necessary to tax away all the benefits and pay them to the creators. It is sufficient to subsidize the creators by enough to ensure production at the socially desirable rate. Patent and copyright laws are both attempts to protect the "property" of the creator and allow him to capture a reasonable rate of return on the investment he has made in his creative activities.

Custom itself is one of the most important barriers to antisocial behavior, or social spillouts. Social ostracism can be a powerful sanction against private activities offensive to neighbors. Tradition itself is often enough to prohibit many negative external effects. A science of manners could indeed be built around the need for people to recognize the effects of their personal actions on others and take care to mitigate those which are most irritating to others and least costly to change.

There is an interaction between manners and laws that affects the freedom that a people can enjoy. Laws and manners are to some extent substitutes. A community that has developed habits against littering does not need antilittering laws. A society in which crime is rare needs few laws against crime. Censorship is unnecessary at any level when good taste prevails.* A system of ethics and the inculcation of socially defensible habits replace coercion and bureaucratic control as a regulating principle of society.

The older, more traditional, and more heavily populated countries, such as England, Japan, and China, out of necessity have developed manners to a higher point than younger, rougher, and less heavily populated countries like the United States and Russia. As a consequence, more regulations are necessary in these societies. But the rub is that the regulations that are imposed may remove from men the responsibility for self-regulation; coercion is not as durable a force as self-discipline arising out of what may be called social self-interest. On these grounds we should expect now to see a deterioration of traditional manners in countries like Britain and, even more, China, which have gone in for greater regimentation and homogenization of society since the Second World War.

Adam Smith was well aware of some of these interactions when he expounded his doctrine of the invisible hand. After all, he had published *The Theory of Moral Sentiments* in 1759, seventeen years before *The Wealth of Nations;* as this suggests, he had tried to develop a theory of social interest long before he had expounded his theory of self-interest.

Insofar as it is to the advantage of society to avoid the harmful effects of overregulation, it is to its advantage to adhere to a system of manners that renders such regulation unnecessary. We shall explore some aspects of this matter in the next and final chapter, "The Cooperative Imperative."

* It can also be dangerous even when good taste does not prevail.

20. *The Cooperative Imperative*

The invisible hand guides decentralized economic society in the direction of the common good in that class of activities that do not involve externalities. But externalities imply unexploited opportunities for profits and hence reflect a disequilibrium situation.

Social organizations can develop to exploit these gains, capturing the gains or profits from coordinated activities by internalizing the externalities. Families form to exploit the externalities inherent in procreation and individual loneliness: men and women are sexual complements. Firms rise to internalize the gains inherent in the greater profitability of the agents of production acting cooperatively rather than in isolation: productive factors are typically economic complements. Governments are formed to exploit the gains from the collective consumption of public services and to establish the rules and regulations systematizing the environment in which private activities are coordinated: private enterprise and legal order are social complements.

The nature of the organization that forms to deal with externalities depends on the legal structure and the traditions of the society as well as on the characteristics of the externality. In countries where the state acts as entrepreneur—which is the case in the Communist countries and those with underdeveloped economies that have opted for the bureaucratic socialist path to planning—the exploitation of new opportunities awaits the decision of the government. Advocates of this path to economic wealth stress the merits of long-range planning for regimenting and mobilizing the resources of society and the superior quality of the decisions of a centralized bureaucracy.

In countries where a large fraction of decisions are left in private hands, on the other hand, as in competitive capitalist countries like the United States, the decision to exploit profitable opportunities for new organizations starts at a lower level and is left to the private initiative of the millions of decentralized would-be entrepreneurs seeking their own private gain. Adherents of this system point to the superior knowledge that exists at a decentralized level, to the greater possibility of exploiting new talents and ideas quickly, and to the enlarged sphere of freedom and personal responsibility that exists for the individual within society.

Quite aside from the legal framework of the society, however, the type of organization that develops depends on the technological characteristics of the externality; certain institutional forms are common to all societies. In the case of the family it is primarily a biological factor that determines the structure of the family nucleus of mother, father, and children, while sociological factors—deriving from tradition and history—determine the proximity and range of the weaker relations of more distant kinship and friendship.

The size of firms is governed by technological and organizational factors. Large steel plants are more efficient than small steel plants, and this characteristic sets a minimum capital requirement for a new steel firm. One firm may control many steel plants at different locations, so that large-scale operations, when they do not conflict with the limits of managerial control, are more prevalent than small-scale operations.

Government, as we have seen, starts within the individual and family and extends up to elaborate centralized hierarchies. Community governments provide services that tend to be specific to local inhabitants; water services, garbage collection, fire prevention, education, and community centers are usually provided by local governments insofar as they are of primary concern to local inhabitants. People are mobile between communities, however, so that the state government and even the Federal government have a stake in education, welfare, and police protection; spillover effects in the form of "brain drain," "poverty drain," and "crime drain" arise between communities. Defense, of course, is needed only for the nation as a whole in countries where the central government is strong enough to prevent civil wars, and for this reason it is the responsibility of the senior government in the land.

The range of externalities is so widespread throughout society that it might be thought that the case for intervention in nearly every sphere of human activity is a compelling one. Indeed this is the argument usually raised by socialists. There are hardly any of our activities that do not, in one way or another, touch upon the public welfare. Even in those spheres of activity that have been jealously guarded as the prerogative of the individual, including the moral and religious education of youth, the size of the family, property rights, and the right to bear arms, what is done has an impact on society as a whole and therefore a bearing on the necessary degree and level of government intervention. If there were only the gains from collective action to consider, and no costs, we would surely all be collectivists now.

Or would we? We could first of all look at the tangible costs of government and the increasing costs of big government. More elaborate hierarchical tiers imply a loss of control; bureaucracy sets in, and big government can accomplish only rather inefficiently many things that can be done efficiently by the local community or the individual. It is hard indeed for a government in Washington to make efficient decisions about local roads in the townships of Illinois or the wilds of the Dakotas because of unfamiliarity with the needs of the local community; it is difficult for a planner in Delhi to decide how many nuts and bolts should be allotted to a factory in Madras. It is on this account far better for the local inhabitants (or entrepreneurs) to make the decisions on the spot and even pay for the roads through local taxes (or for the nuts and bolts out of company funds), since the community residents (or the individual firm) will capture the major benefits of local projects.

Social welfare benefits constitute another case where decisions at the federal level are by themselves unlikely to be efficient. Nationally administered welfare schemes typically set national standards fixed in terms of money. But the cost of living varies in different parts of a country, and a national standard would imply interregional inequities. In the United States, for example, insofar as rents are lower in the Southern states than in the Eastern or Pacific states, welfare standards equalized in dollar terms throughout the country would attract recipients of welfare to the South, where the real benefits would be greater. There is no reason to suppose this migration of the indigent would be efficient. The best that can be done, therefore, is to establish *minimum* national standards (if they are necessary) and exploit the advantages of decentralized decision making for supplementary requirements, to take advantage of tailoring particular situations requiring specialized community knowledge to the specific needs of the inhabitants. This principle has to be balanced against the gains from correcting inequities due to specific locational advantages; there is no reason, for example, why the working inhabitants of California or Florida, both of which are havens for the retired, should bear a disproportionate share of the burden of retirement or old-age pension payments.

A second argument cautioning against excessive government intervention has already been mentioned. A government that intervenes, through the tax system, to offset all the divergencies between social and private rates of return due to externalities may freeze the institutional structure in an inefficient pattern by blunting the signals that guide the social evolution of private groups. The exploitation of the externality requires for efficiency the formation of a new social group but not necessarily a government group. Scientific socialism—that system by which the government puts a tax on every activity yielding external diseconomies and a subsidy on every activity yielding external economies—is theoretically faulty precisely because it ignores the dynamic evolution of the social structure. In the interests of creating a static optimum it discourages the formation of social groups—public or private—that should automatically arise in the absence of intervention. Externalities represent an opportunity and should not be regarded as an unmitigated cost.

There is yet another reason compelling restraint on the part of a community in ceding decentralized powers to higher echelons. Short-run gains can create long-run losses. By allowing the government jurisdiction over matters, which in the short run seem to involve inefficiency when handled informally by the community, society can alter, often to its detriment, the ingrained habits of a community that have taken perhaps generations to learn. This point can be illustrated best by the example of relief payments. It is widely believed that public provision for the needy has reduced private charity (or at least changed its goals), but more important, it has altered the character of the recipients of it. It is one thing for society to arrange to help out the crippled, the handicapped, and the deprived who have suffered from ill luck, misfortune, or great initial handicaps. It is quite another thing to create in healthy individuals the expectation that the government has the responsibility to compensate them for personal actions that have turned out badly. If a man chooses an occupation that later turns out to be an unprofitable one because of innovations or changes in demand-supply conditions, should the government bear the cost of his redirection in another activity? If a sawmill closes down, should government intervene to bring industry back to help the unemployed, or should the unemployed move to another city where jobs are more plentiful? If the price of wheat goes down, should the government subsidize the wheat farmer, or should he accept the fall in price as part of the risk of the market? It is extremely tempting to answer these questions charitably because it is always easier in modern society to adopt the soft view than to take the hard view. But any responsible person who has thought hard about the impact of paternalism on society in the long run cannot escape an uneasy feeling that the short-run gain is purchased at a high long-run cost.

However the questions are answered, it is a fact that government cannot intervene to offset every change that occurs in the market situation of particular individuals without destroying the most powerful incentives for private initiative and personal responsibility. Countries like the United States, Australia, and Canada were founded on the tough-minded cult of rugged individualism in which the major responsibility for individual success or failure rested with a man, his family, and his friends rather than upon society as a whole; and unless this principle is replaced by another principle of equal merit, by one with equal prospects of success, society runs a risk that it will destroy the incentive for human responsibility this principle implies.

Just as a bridge player who is tempted by the attraction of short-run profit to underbid to compensate for a partner who overbids learns that the opposite strategy is the only one that can pay off in the long run if he is likely to play again with the same partner, just as a mother who is tempted to remind her child every time he is in the act of forgetting eventually learns that a continually reminded child can become a forgetful one, so society learns, through collective social action, that long-run wisdom and the hard view are in conflict with short-run wisdom and the soft view. The welfare state in its more developed form can create a society of dependent individuals.*

* This applies even on the international level. The success of the Marshall Plan in Europe owed much to the fact that European countries (through the Organization for European Economic Cooperation) were given the responsibility for supervising and determining the allocation of funds, placing on the aid recipients the blame for any failure. Contrast the success of the European Recovery Program with the troubles of the Alliance for Progress.

The soft view looks at the long run as a sequence of short runs; the hard view looks at the short run as a means to a desirable long run.

These are strong enough grounds to caution against an unlicensed intrusion of government activities in a wide sphere of human activity. But we have not yet come to grips with one of the greatest resistances to government. It is an attitude made up of a man's jealousy of his own freedom, his territorial instincts, and his love of diversity. Unfortunately these concepts —especially freedom—are not easy to define precisely.

To some people freedom is a divine dispensation, a natural birthright of man, like the soul, a gift of God, the symbol of man's separation from other species. Whatever the validity of that concept of the origin of freedom, there is no way of proving or disproving it. It is an approach to life, perhaps worthy of respect, but it is not a scientific answer. It is of no help to us in answering questions about the proper jurisdiction of government activity.

It is tempting to define freedom simply as the absence of constraint on choice. But the moment we develop this theme, we find that all choice involves constraints—all individuals are constrained by limitations on their fields of choice—so that this definition quickly falls to the ground and becomes meaningless.

Still another temptation is to describe freedom as the absence of laws with which an individual disagrees. But this definition is much too strong to be useful. It would imply that only unanimous laws can preserve freedom, and yet we have seen, in a previous chapter, that unanimity is unlikely in a wide variety of choices. A government resting on the unanimity principle would be a government that had little power to exploit the joint neighborhood effects present in a wide range of spheres. For example, a law against a particular crime will not be pleasing to the individual criminal, but it will be a means by which, in an important sense, individuals in society can extend their sphere of safety, which is surely itself a legitimate dimension of freedom.

Freedom might loosely be regarded as the absence of arbitrary coercion. This properly recognizes the need for coercion of some form and focuses attention on the harmful effects of *arbitrary* actions constraining freedom of choice. This definition can be useful as a working definition; it is, however, insufficiently precise for some purposes.

Freedom is a personal thing, and its dimensions cannot be the same for all people. A law that forbids gambling is a constraint on an activity that many in society consider harmless; on the other hand, the existence of gambling establishments in specific local communities may alter the complexion of the society a given group wants to establish; at the least, zoning requirements become necessary. Censorship laws impose a severe constraint on freedom, and yet the absence of such laws, it is claimed, may corrupt youth and initiate the disintegration of the moral basis on which a particular society has been formed. The main issue in censorship is not whether it should exist, but rather at what level it should be enforced—at the individual or family level, community level, or government level.

There is not a single one of these issues that, upon impartial examination, offers an easy solution. What is revealed is the diversity of the interests of man, conflicts between his role as an individual and as a member of society, and a relation between freedom and character. Before society forms, before a constitution is written, the aggregation of individuals about to make a social compact has some conception of the characteristics of the society it wants to create. One society may want unfettered freedom for the fullest expression of artistic and creative endeavor and may do without censorship laws, while another may prefer that the avenues of communication be controlled more strictly in order to promote, self-consciously, a society that reflects the common base of social interest of the initiating group. The Mormons of Utah, the Amish of Pennsylvania, and the Daughters of the American Revolution all have different concepts of what constitutes a good society.

Because of the natural diversity of instinct and character, protection of freedom requires a reasonable *diversity* of laws. A universal law forbidding publication of sexual scenes in novels may be justly condemned as an affront to man's intelligence or his ability to decentralize activities into smaller, more unanimous social groups. Proliferation of laws created by decentralized organs of government enhances freedom, diversity, and—sometimes—productivity. Thus single national laws and regulations may not be efficient if they apply simultaneously to the Detroit mechanic, the Philadelphia lawyer, the Carolina tobacco farmer, the Massachusetts fisherman, the Texas farmhand, and the Oregon lumberjack. As it has been put in a magazine advertisement, "They're not *equal*, they're *individual*. Try to make them all equal by the same regulations and you downgrade them all—you average down when we should build up."

Diversity of laws and regulations can only be achieved in a decentralized society. Decentralization begins with the family, and every family government knows it can control some activities of each member of it, but not all. Overly tyrannical parents can produce children who, as adults, tend to the extremes of impotence or authoritarianism; there is a proper sphere of privacy which even for the child becomes a vital part of his character and without which he would not learn to abandon the dependent role of a child. Any society that values independence of the individual must allow independence to be practiced.

Just as the family heads must limit the authority of their power and allow the child and each other a sphere of privacy, so society has to restrain the exercise of its collective power and leave an area of freedom open to lesser governments and private families or individuals.

One of the great struggles in politics has been the problem of determining the appropriate blend between the forces of decentralization and centralization in demarcating the zones separating those interests that should be left in the hands of the individual, the family, the local community, the state, the federal government, and the sovereign nation. Excessive centralization is an imposition of unnecessary coercion on a wide class of participants in society and has a leveling and homogenizing effect not in the interests of a great society or a creative society; excessive decentralization, on the other hand, can involve anarchy or the failure to capture some of the gains from common social purpose and wider collective endeavor.

It might well be argued that the centralization of big countries has proceeded too far, leaving insufficient scope, in a wide range of activities, for diversity of state and local interests, while the Balkanization of other areas—in Europe and Africa—has been wasteful. Large states have imposed on themselves, on grounds of a single dimension of efficiency, an unnecessarily high degree of uniformity. Despite the greatness of its culture, for example, the United States has probably not been as creative, per capita, as ancient Greece, Renaissance Italy, or even Western Europe in the nineteenth century. The same generalization holds for Russia and China and India (and there are signs that increased homogenization is becoming a modern ethic). On the other hand, centralization has been pitched at the wrong level, in the sense that the strength of national military powers makes supranational power impotent. The United Nations, for example, has no hope of disciplining the Great Powers, so that the problem of preserving peace reduces to a problem of ensuring cooperation among the Great Powers.

The absence of an effective world government points to an "institutional gap" in world society, an externality as yet unexploited. The existence of the externality is made manifest by the spillover effects of one nation's policies upon the welfare of other nations, especially in the sphere of military power but in other areas as well. The gains from exploiting the externality, internalizing it, by creating an effective world government would be nothing less than the reduction of the risk of colossal destruction. And yet a world government with powers to coerce the superpowers (control them without their consent) is virtually inconceivable in the present stage of evolution of world society.

The analogy to the problem of the monetary system discussed in Chapter 15 is clear. The risk of a breakdown in the current international monetary system is, by common agreement, a serious one. And yet the likelihood that a world central bank could be created to correct the deficiencies of the present system is extremely remote. Yet if the countries of the Group of Ten, the Western financial powers, cannot agree among themselves (and the London decision of August, 1967, on a new drawing facility at the IMF does not constitute a genuine agreement), how can it be expected that countries as diverse in ideology as the United States and Russia can agree on preserving the peace?

It is tempting to suggest that self-interest alone is enough to preserve the peace, since neither Russia nor America has an interest in consigning the other or the rest of the world to oblivion. Unhappily for man experience does not bear that happy conjecture out. The First World War is perhaps the best instance of a devastating convulsion which no nation really wanted. We must therefore not look to sheer optimism for a guiding principle of action in a world where coercion at the supranational level is not possible.

One answer, oddly enough, was suggested in the discussion of Adam Smith and the interaction between manners and laws in the previous chapter. It was asserted that laws and regulations may have harmful effects on the evolution of manners and that the spontaneous creation of manners can render laws and regulations unnecessary. We must then ask what manners ought to be created or whose ought to be emulated.

Society, having found the answer to this problem, creates or emulates the required manners, rendering the laws that would have accomplished its purposes unnecessary and sparing itself the excess burden of regulation. The gains from the exchange of magical goods become evident, and metatrade in the form of convention and cooperation becomes possible.

An analogous proposition holds for the world monetary system. The financial powers, being unable to cede to a world central bank monetary sovereignty, can *act as if it existed* and voluntarily adopt those policies a world bank would be directed to adopt if it did exist. We saw in Chapter 15 that this would require that the European powers and Japan take more responsibility for maintaining the price of gold through adjustment of their reserve portfolios and that the United States take more responsibility for the level of world expenditure through its monetary policy.

In the sphere of world politics a similar approach can, with time, become feasible. An effective world government may not prove feasible in the next half century, yet this practical barrier does not mean that study of the policies a world government *should* pursue, if it existed, is a useless endeavor. Following a principle of cooperative simulation, we can ask what directives to national governments a world government, *if it existed,* would advance in the international social interest and then regard the adoption of these policies as a moral imperative. As an ethic, growing out of expediency and the instincts of self-preservation, it would not be a utopian ideal, but a natural expression of the increasingly impatient conscience of mankind, the *cooperative imperative* of our times.